Voices from St. Simons

Personal Narratives of an Island's Past

Also by Stephen Doster

Lord Baltimore: A Novel

Voices from St. Simons
Personal Narratives of an Island's Past

BY STEPHEN DOSTER

John F. Blair, Publisher
WINSTON-SALEM, NORTH CAROLINA

The paper in this book meets the guidelines
for permanence and durability of the Committee on
Production Guidelines for Book Longevity
of the Council on Library Resources.

Cover image courtesy of Joy Fisher, Penny Postcards,
http://www.rootsweb.com/~usgenweb/special/ppcs/ppcs.html

Library of Congress Cataloging-in-Publication Data
Voices from St. Simons : personal narratives of an island's past / edited
by Stephen Doster.
p.   c.
Includes bibliographical references and index.
ISBN-13: 978-0-89587-357-6 (alk. paper)
ISBN-10: 0-89587-357-5 (alk. paper)
1. Saint Simons Island (Ga. : Island)—History.   I. Doster, S. M. G. (Stephen M. G.), 1959– II. Title: Voices from Saint Simons.
F292.G58V65 2008
975.8'742—dc22   2007050758

In memoriam

Peter Eric Hansen

Contents

Preface

When a hurricane washes over the barrier islands of the Georgia coast, the results are immediate and clearly visible. With time, the action of wind and water changes the islands' physical characteristics to the extent that one's ancestors might find them largely unrecognizable or at the very least disorienting. For the most part, a disappearing coastline takes place gradually, almost imperceptibly, one tide at a time.

The same thing applies to the way of life, the culture, and the people who inhabit a place. The forces that bring them into existence and usher them into oblivion are equally slow acting and just as imperceptible. However, in the past fifty years, a hurricane in the form of resort and residential development has sped up this process in the Golden Isles area of the Georgia coast, particularly on St. Simons Island. The effect has been a gradual erosion of a way of life in which ox-drawn carts, summer cottages, and small mercantile stores have given way to expensive automobiles, oversized condos, and upscale shops.

These narratives represent an oral archaeological dig. The accounts of days gone by allow readers to sift through the layers of new development to reveal a time and place largely preserved only in the minds of those with long memories. It is in those in-between places not yet bulldozed and built on where you will find people who recount less tame, more exhilarating days when "haints" and larger-than-life figures roamed the coast. Their stories, presented here, represent a demarcation, a line in the sand, between old days and new ways.

Historians have assigned specific eras to St. Simons Island and the Golden Isles: the Native American era, the Spanish missions era, the colonial (English) era, the plantation era, the Civil War era, and the mill era. Each period was distinct, and each vanished slowly, to be replaced by a new one. Two new eras—the resort era and the residential era—represent a transition from post–Civil War days to the present. Some historians would pay a king's ransom to interview anyone who lived during the mill days and earlier eras. But that's impossible, so they rely on primary source materials (diaries, manuscripts) and secondary sources (articles, newspapers, textbooks) to piece together the past. But what if one could have all three—primary and secondary sources, as well as firsthand accounts by people who lived during a given era?

That is essentially the purpose of this book—to preserve the legacy of the area while those who still recall it are able to share their memories. Unfortunately, one of those featured here, Evelyn Oliver, passed away just three months after being interviewed. So it is with a sense of urgency that these recollections have been recorded. Once these people are gone, their undocumented memories will go with them.

The impetus for recording these narratives was hearing local residents utter the famous sentiment that someone should have recorded so-and-so's recollections before she died. After more than a few decades of hearing this, I concluded they were right, that indeed someone ought to record those memories. Not too long after that, I read the obituary of a former elementary-school teacher, Mrs. Lefty Butler. I thought Mrs. Butler, one of the few credible witnesses of the island's foremost ghost, Mary de Wanderer, had died years before. In fact, she lived to be more than a hundred years old.

Following her death, I began to contact people with deep roots in the Golden Isles. As it turned out, those with the deepest roots were the descendants of planters and slaves. Five of the people in this collection are direct descendants of well-known planters who owned plantations in and around St. Simons Island. Seven interviewees are direct descendants of slaves; six of them descend from slaves who lived and worked on area plantations. In some respects, their collective tales are a model for how people of mixed races should get along with one another.

Black-white relations have been referred to as "a delicate dance." On these pages, readers will see blacks and whites interacting over several centuries in ways that may seem unthinkable by those who are out of step. Descendants of slaves and descendants of masters have lived here in relative harmony, bound by geography and the shared experiences of slavery, hurricanes, the Civil War, Prohibition, the Great Depression, and World War II, all of which represented both opportunities and threats to their way of life.

This dance is perhaps best illustrated by Captain Charles Stevens and his servant, Randolph Abbott, who served with him in the Confederate army. Years later, during the Depression, Randolph's nephew, Robert Abbott, a self-made millionaire, sent money to Stevens's descendants living at Frederica. In another, better-known incident, Neptune Small, a servant of the King family of Retreat Plantation, sought and found Lordy King's body on the battleground at Fredericksburg and brought it back to Georgia for burial. The descendants of both the masters and slaves of these families tell their stories in the following pages.

Readers are cautioned not to come away with the notion that black-white relations have always been good and that slaves were content with life on the plantation. It is certainly possible to cherry-pick excerpts from the interviews to make that case. However, history and a close reading of these narratives prove otherwise. Those who were interviewed, both black and white, chose not to discuss in detail the dark side of slavery or Jim Crow.

In some respects, the narratives reveal a plot of ground that time forgot, a place where longtime residents talk about the late 1800s and early 1900s as you or I would discuss events of the last decade. Wherever appropriate, family correspondence, newspaper clippings, and book excerpts are used as chapter notes to reinforce or expand on the interviewees' comments. This supporting information is also used to corroborate or clarify interviewees' references to historical people and events with which readers may not be familiar.

It should be noted that readers won't learn everything that was shared by the interviewees. In many instances, they requested that I not repeat something—secrets among locals—which I have honored.

These interviews were conducted in person and over the phone over a period of five years. The first thing that struck me as I listened was the interviewees' long reach into the past as they summoned up firsthand accounts of people and events I had only read about in history books. It was an unexpected surprise to find that so much of what they recalled was supported by old newspapers, biographies, and historical texts. Discrepancies between one person's recollections and another's are few and minor. In some instances, I have recorded word pronunciations verbatim in order to preserve the Gullah/Geechee dialect that still survives on the coast.

The first nine chapters alternate the oral recollections of slave descendants and planter descendants. These chapters are followed by the narratives of longtime residents whose equally compelling stories provide unique insights from diverse perspectives. As much as possible, I tried not to direct the thoughts of those being interviewed. Other than the staple opening—"When and where were you born?"—I encouraged the interviewees to discuss topics of interest or importance to them in a free-form style that makes each narrative distinct. Readers may discern common threads woven among the narratives, the result of lives and events overlapping in an insular island environment.

This book is not intended to be a comprehensive history of the area. It presents the reflections of a cross-section of ordinary people who lived during extraordinary times.

Ultimately, the narratives are a story of a tiny geographical location and the people who have inhabited it—an Indian hunting ground alternately occupied and/or invaded by Spanish missionaries, British settlers, Spanish warships, planters, the Union army, and the United States Navy. More recently, the Golden Isles have become a playground for tourists and the focus of developers. Overdevelopment is an issue on which most of those interviewed comment.

The forces that brought about the current state of rapid development have roots in the late 1800s, when local entrepreneurs like Mallery King (the ancestor of Harry Aiken, Jr.) began selling ocean lots and making plans to attract tourists to St. Simons. Upon the completion of the causeway in 1924, easy access to the island ensured the development of new neighborhoods and repeat tourist visits. Many of those visitors, such as Edwin Fendig's family, chose to settle on the island permanently. Both trends—tourism and residency—have increased exponentially over the years, with each new generation leaving its mark in the form of more and larger homes and shopping centers.

The book's title reflects the fact that each interviewee has either lived on St. Simons or has some intimate connection to it. The island's significance to Georgia and American history can be measured by the number of books and articles written about it and by the number of historical markers scattered across a relatively small area. Mile for mile, the island may harbor the densest concentration of historical events on the East Coast.

Sooner or later, everything becomes history. But not everything is historic. The objective is to preserve that which will one day be of historical significance. When it comes to oral history, the challenge is in identifying what might be of importance and recording that knowledge while those who possess it are still alive. I hope these narratives succeed in doing that.

A Brief History of the Golden Isles

For anyone not familiar with the Golden Isles of Georgia, a short history will make the text more readable. What follows is five hundred years' worth of history, much of which the interviewees conjure up in their recollections of people and places past and present.

The Golden Isles, so named for the golden hue of their surrounding marshes, are barrier islands on the southeast coast of Georgia. They were occupied by Timucua, Guale, and other Indian tribes before the arrival of the Spanish in the 1500s. The Spanish established missions on the islands and the mainland from St. Augustine to South Carolina. Missions were established on an island the Indians called Asao, or Guadalquini. The Spanish named it San Simon, later Anglicized to St. Simons.

Over the years, the Timucua and Guale tribes disappeared due to overwork, disease, enslavement, and tribal warfare, and their lands were taken over by Creeks and Cherokees. Indian uprisings were partially responsible for Spain's retreat to Florida, where a series of missions between St. Augustine and the Florida Panhandle had also been established.

In the 1700s, the British, under James Oglethorpe, established a colony that served as a buffer between South Carolina and Spanish Florida. Oglethorpe, befriended by the Creeks, established towns at Savannah, Darien (occupied by Scottish Highlanders), and Frederica on St. Simons Island. Oglethorpe brought two young men of the cloth, John and Charles Wesley, who administered—mostly in vain—to the colonists' spiritual needs. Historic Christ Church, located near the old town of Frederica, took root with the Wesleys, who would later found Methodism.

In 1742, Oglethorpe repelled an invasion of thirty-four Spanish ships carrying two thousand men from Havana and St. Augustine. The Battle of Gully Hole Creek, near what is now Christ Church, and the Battle of Bloody Marsh, near what is now the St. Simons airport, were small but decisive encounters that marked the end of Spain's claim to lands north of the St. Mary's River on the Georgia-Florida border. With the threat of Spanish conquest gone, the town of Frederica was largely abandoned, and St. Simons lay relatively dormant until men such as John Couper, Thomas Butler King, and Pierce Butler established rice and cotton plantations in the area. Several of these planters are buried at Christ Church Cemetery.

In 1803, a ship named *The York* bearing Ebo (a.k.a. Ibo or Igbo) slaves from Africa landed on St. Simons. The Ebo rebelled, a number of them drowning themselves while chanting, "The water brought us, and the water will take us away."

After the Civil War, large sawmill operations were built on the southwest end of St. Simons at Gascoigne Bluff. Trees felled on the island and logs rafted downriver from central Georgia were cut and shipped by schooners to New England and Europe. Blacks, many of whom worked at the lumbermills, clustered in three main settlements on the island: Harrington, South End, and Jewtown (quite possibly the most politically incorrect name for a community in America), so named by the blacks in reference to a Jewish merchant named Levison who built a store that catered to the mill workers.

Before the turn of the twentieth century, the Golden Isles had become a winter retreat for some of America's wealthiest families. Jekyll Island, known to the Indians as Ospo and renamed by James Oglethorpe in honor of his friend Sir Joseph Jekyll, was purchased in 1886 by a group of men who organized the Jekyll Island Club. The membership roster included names such as Gould, Astor, Vanderbilt, Rockefeller, Morgan, Goodyear, Macy, and Pulitzer. Not to be outdone, the Carnegie family turned Cumberland Island into its own private playground.

In the early 1900s, Howard Coffin, a Hudson Motor Company executive, attended Savannah's automobile road races. Coffin would later stay to purchase Sapelo Island and a smaller island overrun with goats. He and his cousin Alfred Jones renamed the second property Sea Island and turned it into an internationally acclaimed resort. (In 2004, Sea Island hosted the G8 summit.) Due to mounting debt in the 1930s, Coffin reluctantly sold Sapelo to tobacco heir R. J. Reynolds, Jr., who turned the island into a private hunting reserve.

A local engineer named Fernando J. Torras oversaw construction of a four-mile causeway and five bridges that linked St. Simons Island to the mainland. The causeway, completed in 1924, would prove a lifeline to islanders, as well as the catalyst of change that attracted vacationers, many of whom would become full-time residents.

In 1927, just months after Charles Lindbergh's thirty-three-hour flight across the Atlantic, the city of Brunswick, along with Howard Coffin, backed a young aviator named Paul Redfern in his attempt to fly solo from the Sea Island beach to Rio de Janeiro,

Brazil, a fifty-five-hour marathon. Though he was last seen off the coast of Venezuela, and though a dozen search parties never found his plane, Redfern is credited as being the first aviator to solo the Caribbean.

World War II brought a new invasion to the islands in the form of the United States Navy, which set up operations to protect the coast from German U-boats. Thousands of laborers who poured into the area to work on the Liberty ships remained after the war, adding to the local population.

Numerous publications, taken in their entirety, thoroughly weave together the history of Georgia's coast (see the bibliography for a partial list). In particular, *Early Days of Coastal Georgia*, by Orrin Sage Wightman and Margaret Davis Cate, and *Old Mill Days*, by Abbie Fuller Graham, tell the story of the Golden Isles from their founding through the 1930s. The narratives that follow pick up that thread and continue this story from the 1930s to the present.

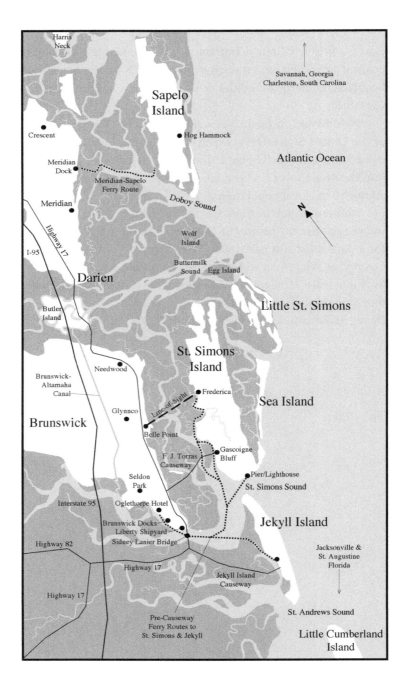

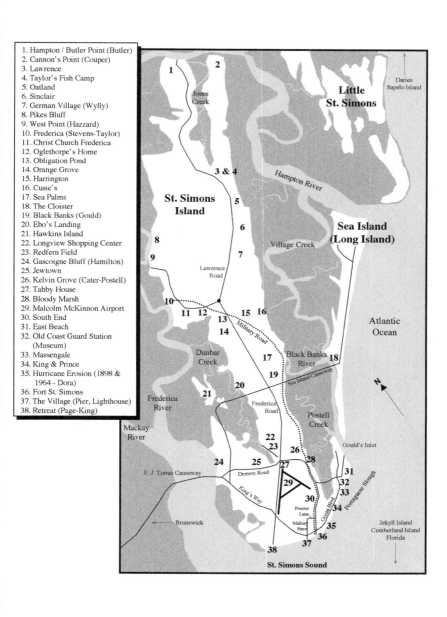

Darien
Sapelo Island

Little
St. Simons

Jones
Creek

Hampton River

3 & 4

St. Simons
Island

Sea Island
(Long Island)

Village Creek

Lawrence
Road

Atlantic
Ocean

Military Road

Dunbar
Creek

Black Banks
River

Sea Island Causeway

Frederica
River

Frederica
Road

Postell
Creek

Mackay
River

Gould's Inlet

F. J. Torras Causeway

Demere Road

King's Way

Portuguese Slough

Brunswick

Proctor
Lane

Mallory
Street

Ocean Blvd

Jekyll Island
Cumberland Island
Florida

St. Simons Sound

Acknowledgments

Virginia Hobson Hicks, Audrey Grovner, Alcinea Follins, Mack and Leslie Mattingly, and Shirley Hunter put me in touch with several people whose narratives appear in this book. Local author and historian Patricia Cofer Barefoot was an invaluable resource in recommending other people who agreed to share their stories. Catherine Cate provided a number of Cate family documents and photographs. Cynthia Miles, Gail Mobley, Bobby Haven, and Betty Oliver also provided images of narrators. Cary Knapp of the Brunswick–Glynn County Library and George Dorrance researched archives that corroborated much of the information presented in these pages. Allen and Angie Burns contributed local news clippings dating to the late 1800s. Devon Boan, director of the Honors Program at Belmont University, provided support during a crucial phase in this book's development. My mother, Majorie Terry Doster, motivated me to complete the narratives in a timely fashion. Lynn Stoudt of the Georgia Historical Society provided guidance in the citation of various texts. Dewey Benefield, president of the Fort Frederica Association, graciously granted permission to use text and images from *Early Days of Coastal Georgia* and *A Voyage to Georgia*. Libby Hogan, chairman of the board of directors of the St. Simons Public Library, Inc., granted permission to use material from *Old Mill Days: St. Simons Mills, Georgia, 1874–1908*. I thank all of these people.

I especially thank my wife, Anne, for her encouragement and for her editing of my editing.

Most of all, I thank everyone who took the time to share their thoughts and memories on the pages that follow.

To the people of the Golden Isles and the Georgia coast—this is your story.

Voices from St. Simons

*Personal Narratives of
an Island's Past*

Sadie Marie Jackson Ryals, 1944

Sadie Marie Jackson Ryals

Sadie Ryals, born in 1924, is the oldest of thirteen children raised in a small community just north of Darien, Georgia. She is the descendant of slaves who worked the rice fields for Pierce Butler, a prominent Philadelphian who inherited plantations near Darien and on St. Simons Island. Butler married the renowned English actress Fanny Kemble. From her brief visit to the Butler estates, Kemble penned Journal of a Residence on a Georgian Plantation *in 1838–1839, published in 1863. Margaret Davis Cate writes in* Early Days of Coastal Georgia *that Kemble's journal was said to have "caused more criticism of the South than any book that was ever written except Uncle Tom's Cabin,"[1] and that the journal was credited with raising antislavery sentiment among European nations at a time when the South was trying to enlist their support. Kemble's*

views on slavery earned her the label of "violent abolitionist," which descendants of area planters still talk about (see the Eleanor Stiles Cate narrative). In a coincidental twist of fate, Kemble's reaction to Mrs. Ryals's ancestors' plight may have helped bring about the end of slavery.

Darien is the home port of a shrimp-boat fleet. For decades, Mrs. Ryals's family members have worked on the boats at a high personal price—the sea has claimed the lives of her husband, a brother, and a son.

In this narrative, it is evident that the 1803 incident at Ebo's Landing still weighs heavily on Mrs. Ryals's mind. She recalls the days when childbirth took place in the home, when children slept six to a bed on mattresses stuffed with Spanish moss, and when black children walked the ten miles to public school. She recounts fanning rice, the evolution of her church from a "bush harbor," and attending services led by Father Divine and Bishop C. M. "Sweet Daddy" Grace, two early 1900s messianic evangelists. Mrs. Ryals also recalls Dr. Buzzard, a famous root doctor, or conjurer, and McIntosh County's infamous Thomas Poppell, the last of the old-time Southern sheriffs.

Just a good old-fashioned meeting
Back in good old-fashioned days
When those good old-fashioned people
Dressed in good old-fashioned ways.

Whiskered men wore jean britches
Homemade socks and brogan shoes
Women wore their checkered aprons
And their hair did up in queue.

Just some good old-fashioned singing
And it did me good to hear
Good old-fashioned people shouting,
"Halleluiah, I'm going there."

Go down, Moses
Way down in Egypt land
Tell old Pharaoh
To let my people go.

I've heard this poem since I was a child. I was born on Smith Road, right in Crescent, Georgia, August 31, 1924. My mother's maiden name was Frances Carolyn Livingston. She was from Crescent, Georgia. She was born May 26, 1903. Her parents were Abe and Sarah Livingston. Sarah was Indian. She had hair way down her back. Pretty black hair. I was the only granddaughter of the Livingstons born in that house.

I was the oldest one of thirteen head, so I came up kind of harder than them. My mother had twin boys after I had my oldest child. I saw Audrey, one of my younger sisters, come out of my mama's womb, September 19, 1941. We had a midwife. She took sick, and I had to help bring her into this world. I dropped Audrey's navel string. We had to put bands on the baby. Had to burn white cloth and put it on the navel until that navel rotten. When the navel string drop, then you put a band on the baby. When the baby grows, you keep tightening it. We had them great big long pins like that to band the little body up to strengthen their back. I had all my babies at home with a midwife.

We used to bury the caul [the membrane enclosing a fetus]. If you didn't bury the caul, the child might see ghosts. We had to bury that stuff in the yard. Sometimes, the caul looks like a thin membrane. Sometimes, people born with a caul are born little ministers and stuff like that.

I don't know what place it was, but they [slave traders] brought the older ones [Africans] over on a ship. There was two white people buying the Negro slaves. They called them slaves "the Butler niggers." That's what they used to call them. On Butler Island. See that brick chimney? Right there. That was a rice plantation. The old ancestors were from Africa. They buy them like they're buying animals.

They'd be in the fields. The only way they could communicate with one another was through songs. They couldn't talk to one another. They didn't allow them to get an education. Now, I don't know nothing 'cause I ain't never seen no slaves out in the field. Just what my fore-parents told me.

First, they called us "black." No, first thing was "niggers." Next thing was "Negroes." Next thing was "colored." Then from "colored" to "African-American." I wasn't born in Africa. I prefer to be called a Negro.

When they brought the slaves over, they landed at Dunbar Creek on St. Simons Island. All the black people chained themselves together. They were singing the song about, "Before I be a slave, I'll be buried in my grave. Go home to my Lord and be at rest." Every time I go down to St. Clair subdivision, I think about [how] those slaves chained themselves together, and all of them drowned. That's right. Right there in Dunbar Creek. There's not a day I go onto St. Simons I don't think about how they did them people, did us.

It's a very sacred place. Like Bloody Marsh. When it rains, they say you could go to Bloody Marsh and see the blood.

The people that bought the slaves, they had communication [intercourse] with the maids and had babies by them. And you see a lot of them look like they're really white. Black women had babies for white men. That was before my time. But they said their father was white.

We had an uncle at Scott Hill, where we were raised up at, named after the Scott family. My grandmother Sarah's maiden name was Scott. We used to have kids come to spend the night with us, three to the head and three to the foot. We wasn't blessed with no nice mattress to sleep on. Our mattress was packed with moss. And you slept on that until it got hard, then we opened that mattress up. You'd take the moss and tease it. You pull it apart. Just stuff it back in. They used to take a long stick, and take and wind it and pull the moss down from the tree. We had all our friends come over and stay for the weekend. Now, all the kids want a room to themselves.

We used to have a lot of house parties at my mama's house. We had a piano. Men used to come play it. And then we'd go to different people's houses. This man played the guitar, Mr. Lawrence Pinkney. He was from Meridian. We danced and had a good time. My house would be crowded. I had the best time of my life over there on St. Simons Island. There was a big club named the Blue Inn by the fire station by the airport. And the Tropicana.

When they built the causeway to St. Simons, you used to pay ten cents. My mom used to take us as little children. They had to pay ten cents for each kid. They used to hide us under their foot. That's the truth I'm telling.

I worked for J. C. Pitts the whole time he had a [car] dealership down in Brunswick. I worked for him when they first moved there, down on Fifteenth Street on the beach, and then they built a new home up there in the Island Club. They moved out of that house back down on Eighth Street, in[to] a two-story house on East Beach. I worked right on Eighth Street. The Schaefers were on the corner. I was thinking about her the other day because I used to check on her a lot.

They call us Geechees. But I don't call myself that. But you want to hear some Gullah talk,[2] go down in Carolina, around Ridgeland and Beaufort. You can't understand nothing those people say. We

Sadie Marie Jackson Ryals, 1999

really don't speak English like we supposed to speak.

A lot of people used to do that root stuff. Back there, we didn't have no doctors. We had herb doctors like Mr. Lucius Armstrong. When we got sick, my mom sent to him to get some medicine. Medicine used to be made from a bush in the yard called jusimoak [or jusimoke, an herbal remedy used by Cherokees]. They go out in the woods and dig sassifax [sassafras] root, too. They were for fevers. And that draw the root to get all that green stuff after the baby was born. And then we draw catnip tea. That's a bush growing in the yard with a bunch of spreads. We feed that to the baby.

A whole lot of people used roots to do people in. Back then, they really believed in it. They tell me a whole lot of them go now to Carolina. They still believe in that stuff up there. They told us back then there used to be a man who made a buzzard row his boat. I don't know anything about that, but that's what they told me—Dr. Buzzard. I ain't never seen him.

My mother went to Todd School, where the post office in Darien is now. My mama used to be very sick. She had asthma. Most times, I had to stay out of school. I was the class of '39. That's where you graduated from the eleventh grade. It didn't go to the twelfth when I was in school. Later, they added the twelfth. I graduated from Hudson Public School in the eighth grade. Then I went on to Todd-Grant School in Darien, Georgia. I walked from Meridian to school. We had to walk the whole way [approximately ten miles] if we couldn't catch a ride, like on R. K. Hopkins' gas truck. And we were at school on time. We took shortcuts through the woods, and we'd pick up all our friends and walk there and get to school on time. School started at eight or nine. They used to make us hot dogs and sauerkraut. A little confectionary was across from the school. We'd go over there and get a sweet roll and a big Mr. Goodbar candy for a nickel. I left in the eleventh grade. That's as far as we went. Todd-Grant is now Mackinesh [McIntosh] Academy. Professor Grant was our relative.

They had school buses for the white kids to ride on. They went to Darien High. But the black kids had to walk. My baby boy was the first and only black boy that finished Darien High when there was freedom of choice. His name is Ernest Lee Ryals. He is a minister, plus he teaches at the Job Corps in Brunswick. He has twenty-five years of military in the army.

When I came up, if you did something wrong, anybody could whip you. Now, police don't want you to whip your own children. No respect for grown people. You had to respect the elderly. I taught my children the same way. I raised those kids in fear of just me and the good Lord. I taught them to respect people, and when they needed a whipping, they got it! That's right.

They took prayer out of the schools. The law going to tell you, you raising your kids and feeding them every day and night, and they going to tell you what you can't do to your child? Every morning, we had to pray. Prayer, morning before school starts. They called it "devotion." Pledge of Allegiance to the flag and prayer. And then go to the different classes. After they integrated, then that's when they started all this mess. I blame the ministers. You mean all these ministers, they're going to stand and let one white woman take prayer out of school? No way!

We used to have plays. I was in all of them. We put on a play, *Pepping Up the PTA*, where we dressed like little school kids. I used to sing a lot.

My daddy's name was Charlie Jackson, Sr. His mother was Miley Jackson. My grandfather Abe Livingston had a farm. They had potatoes and corn, and we used to have to dig potatoes. Every year, he would fix all his land and have a big New Year's party. Cook red peas in the wash pot. Cousin Vi—Viola Palmer—would bake pineapple layer cake. We had apple trees, peaches, and pears on Scott Hill, where we grew up. Loquats, cumquats, tangerines. There was a whole lot of love back then. Because everybody was looking out for people. There weren't drugs and all that going on.

Anyway, we were never deprived of food because Daddy always had a hundred-pound sack of rice he bought from the store. We had a big rice field. We planted rice behind where we lived. Everybody had a rice field, and everybody helped each other. When it was time to harvest the rice, we had to strip them, put it in a mortar, and beat it. And then we had great big old fans and something like a big block, and that block was carved out. We'd take that big block and put it in the backyard. And we'd fan the rice up and down to separate it from the husk.

There was a white lady down here who used to grits the corn. We used to take it down to Mrs. Donnelly, and they would grind the corn using a mule to turn the stone for us to have grits. Just like cane grinding.

All the men did around here was shrimp fishing and pulpwood. That's all they did. My daddy was a shrimp fisherman out of Valona. We were raised up on fish, oyster, and crab. Daddy's boat was the *Captain Hunter*. They'd go out on the ocean and come back every evening.

My husband was the captain of a shrimp trawler. The first boat he got was named the *Bill Bailey*. He was in World War II in Italy. He came out of the military in '42. Then my brother was stationed in Germany during that same time. He came back in October of '51. He went out on a shrimp boat and got drowned. It came up a storm, and it burst the boat open. They found the captain's body all the way up there to Sunbury [north of Darien]. But they never found my brother up 'til this day.

My husband fished out of Tampa down in [the Gulf of] Mexico. He got drowned in 1965. He was on a big shrimp trawler out of Tampa. This particular night, a Thursday in April 1965, they called me and told me the boom on the back of the boat knocked him out of the boat, and where they were fishing, they don't have no bottom. Never found him. Never found my husband. Up until this day, almost forty years. And I raised those kids by myself. I had four children. My son Bubba—Abraham, Jr.—died in my house on my birthday, 31st of August 1996. My oldest son got drowned in 1963, the same year that President Kennedy got assassinated. I lose my son the 23rd of March 1963, and President Kennedy got assassinated in November of '63. I think I cried like his [Kennedy's] wife. He really did a lot for the black folks. People around here used to get fifty cent a day cutting lawns and stuff like that. When President Roosevelt brought in the WPA, then that's the time poor black people got something to eat.

Back then, the guys couldn't come to your house and stay all night. They had to leave at a certain time. I was married twice. I married a Mackinesh [McIntosh]. Sam McIntosh was my first husband. I married Abraham Ryals, my second husband. The first time, I had two sons, and my mom kept my sons along with her. I lived in New York and stayed a couple of years at 2894 Eighth Avenue in Harlem. I worked for the Rockmores. They were Jews. They had their store on Riverside Drive in New York City. They lived in New Rochelle. I took the train out there every day. I had a lot of relatives in New York. When I got my divorce from my first husband, they gave me six dollars apiece for two kids. I came back from New York in Christmas of 1947 and married my second husband in March of 1948. Train travel was nice. It was as fast as we go by car now.

Do I remember Sheriff Poppell?[3] I've known him all my life. Tom Poppell's father, Ad Poppell, was the high sheriff in Darien. And if someone, a black person, killed somebody, he was too scared to go arrest them. He'd send my grandfather Abe Livingston to go arrest them. The sheriff was a scary [scared] white man. He never went to arrest nobody.

When Tom Poppell came along, everybody was crazy about Tom because Tom let a lot of people off the hook. He was a good sheriff. A lot of people didn't like him, but he was a good man. When it was time for the election, he would feed them all that moonshine. Sheriff 'til he died! Lot of people got oranges and white potatoes when a semi truck turned over. Somebody would let them know when a truck wrecked, and everybody would go out there and get some. He was really good to the black people, as far as I know. He would always help them in a lot of ways. A whole lot of cases came up since Tom died for people who thought they were off the hook.

One thing about Mackinesh [McIntosh] County, the black and white people got along real good. In our county, the blacks and the whites always got along real good.

I went to Prospect Baptist Church. The old historic church where I was baptized when I was seven years old burned down in '84. This Prospect Baptist Church is new. I will soon be a church secretary a third time. That church was first started with bush harbor [brush arbor]. My grand-uncle-in-law, Tony Armstrong, cut the first bush to mark the spot of the church. He fell down on his knees and prayed. He was the one who named the church Prospect. They were serving under bush harbor—like a palmetto tent. That's what they called a bush harbor. When I was fourteen, I was elected secretary of that church, and served as secretary until I got married when I was seventeen years old. Then I went away to live to Meridian. Then, later, they called me back a second time, and I served twenty-two years.

I used to live in Savannah. I knew Father Divine and Daddy Grace.[4] I went to their church. They roll that carpet out, and he didn't touch no sand. They roll that carpet out when he's getting out of his car. Lord, they had a band at Daddy Grace church in Savannah. It sounded like you was in heaven! That's right. Playing them big horns. People worshiped them like they had them for their gods.

There was this guy, Washboard Jones. Had that great big old drum, and we'd just dance all around everywhere. "When the saints go marching in . . ." Father Divine had this big place on Victory Drive near Ogeechee Road.

I lived at 747 East Bolton Street [in Savannah]. I was a maid of Miss A. D. Strohbar, who owned the sugar refinery in Savannah. I worked down on Thirty-fifth Street. They had a little girl, and everybody thought that Susan was his grandchild because he was an old man when she got that baby. I was a little maid standing in a white thing around my head and my black uniform and my white apron. I was the first one took her out of the ambulance when they brought her home. My aunt was the head cook the latter part of 1944 and '45, during the war. I never forgot when those soldiers used to come to Savannah, and then when the song came out about, "When the light goes on again all over the world." That song meant, when the boys come home again all over the world.

Years ago, they hang a black lady on an oak tree right in Darien. While they were hanging her, she said, "As long as Darien exists, there will never be nothing. It will bloom up and go down." The tree died. That tree was right there where you come out on 99 and Highway 17. Jailhouse across there, right in that square. They say she was from Sapelo [Island].

Some of the best times I ever had was over there on Sapelo. Going over there to church. I had a sister-in-law taught over there. She stayed over there the whole week and come home at the end of the week. They don't have no school on Sapelo now. *Anna Marie.* That's the boat that Reynolds' [R. J. Reynolds, Jr.'s] wife gave them over there.

You go on down to Harris Neck [north of Darien], straight on down, all the way down to the river. The government had this big strip of land, an airfield at Harris Neck. The government put the blacks on some other old place. They relocated all of them in a little huddle on the right-hand side going into Harris Neck. They almost stopped the black people from burying over there. They said the government was going to give the black people their land back after the war—World War II—ceased. A lot of blacks went to jail for their land, claiming the government took it. They ain't never got it back. They just gave up. They do let the black people bury at their cemetery. The white folks own all that plantation. They got dream homes.

Ooh, Jesus. They got some homes.

NOTES

1. Orrin Sage Wightman and Margaret Davis Cate, *Early Days of Coastal Georgia* (St. Simons Island, Ga.: Fort Frederica Association, 1955), 59.

2. Wightman and Cate, *Early Days of Coastal Georgia*, 205. According to the authors, the terms Geechee and Gullah "were used to designate Negroes who spoke a very poor grade of English. Living on . . . very large rice plantations, they saw very little of white people since the plantation master and his family, in an effort to escape malaria fever, left the plantation in summer. . . . Because of this lack of contact with white people, these rice-field Negroes developed a jargon all their own which bore little resemblance to the English language and which, to a stranger, is like a foreign language."

3. Melissa Faye Greene, *Praying for Sheetrock* (New York: Fawcett Columbine, 1991), xi, xiii. Greene writes that the entrenched authority in the area at that time "was not numberless white men, generals, captains of industry, and vast hierarchies of elected and appointed officials: it was one white man, Sheriff Tom Poppell." She quotes Georgia Bureau of Investigation special agent Harry Coursey's local description: "McIntosh County is pretty country and it's got some nice people, but it's the most different place I've ever been to in my life."

4. http://beachonline.com/oldtime.htm, accessed September 2006. The Web site gives this capsule biography: "Born on a rice plantation near Savannah, Georgia, Father Major Jealous Divine (a.k.a. George Baker) founded the Peace Mission movement. During the Great Depression he led anti-lynching campaigns, instituted economic cooperatives, and organized political action against racial discrimination." http://www.savannahnow.com/stories/092698/ACCuhopconvocation.html, accessed September 2006. According to this Web site, "Bishop Charles M. Grace, founder of the United House of Prayer For All People, was affectionately called 'Sweet Daddy' Grace by his followers. Daddy Grace preached revival in a Pentecostal tradition that included brass shout bands and public baptisms."

Eleanor Stiles Cate, circa 1930

Eleanor Stiles Cate

Mrs. Cate is a direct descendant of John Couper, a colonial planter who corresponded with another well-known planter of that era, Thomas Jefferson. Couper's lavish hospitality drew guests from all over the country and from Europe to his St. Simons Island home. Among them was Aaron Burr, who visited in 1804 after his duel that resulted in the death of Alexander Hamilton. Eleanor Stiles Cate is also a relative of Juliet Gordon Low, founder of the Girl Scouts of America.

Mrs. Cate was present at the dedication of the causeway linking St. Simons Island to the mainland, and she was there when Paul Redfern left the Sea Island beach on his ill-fated attempt to be the first to fly solo to Rio de Janeiro.

Her family once owned Sea Island, now among the most exclusive properties on the East Coast. The family sold the island for five hundred dollars. These days, the land there routinely sells for two to three million per lot.

Mrs. Cate's story is that of Southern aristocracy struggling to survive in the face of hurricanes, the Civil War, Reconstruction, and the Depression. She recalls the days when grocers came to your door and streetcars were common in Southern towns. She remembers vacationing on St. Simons when the only way to get there was by boat. And she recalls landing at Frederica—when it was still a town—to bury her Confederate veteran uncle at Christ Church.

My name is Eleanor Stiles Cate. I was born in the house at 911 Union Street, Brunswick, Georgia, on August 10, 1913. My parents were John Couper Stiles and Eleanor Burdett. My sister, Margaret, was five years older than me, and my brother was five years younger. My mother's people came from New York City. I believe they had a linen shop there. My father was with the Clyde Shipping Company. They had a warehouse office here in Brunswick, and he and Mother lived in Charleston for a while. Mother loved it because she had a stateroom. It was a nice ship ride, except my older sister was just about four years old, and she wouldn't let Mother go out on deck. She was terrified of the water. Mother had to stay in the stateroom with her until they got back to Brunswick.

Then the Depression came, and my father lost his job. We didn't have too much for a while. But everyone else was in the same fix, so it didn't worry us. For clothes, there were plenty of clothing stores around. But you had to have the money to get them. And I had a rich cousin in New York, which was wonderful, because she sent my sister and me her clothes that she had stopped wearing. They were brand-new for us, so we got along fine. She was married to Angier Biddle Duke at one time.

We didn't shop for groceries. When I was small, a black man had a horse and wagon, and he would come up to the house and yell, "Groceries!" or whatever he had. Our cook, Henrietta, would go out with a basin, and Mother would get what she wanted. And we had the fish man, too, who would yell, "Fish!" which were strung on a marsh rack. It looked so pretty. Our milk was delivered to us. There was a delicatessen downtown that also delivered to us. And we had a garden in back.

Henrietta was a former slave. I remember Father correcting her about something, and she said, "Mr. Cate, I was not a house slave. I worked in the fields." Wasn't that horrible? That's one thing I'm ashamed of. Mercy!

My father went to the Episcopal church. I went to St. Francis Xavier Church, which was torn down and replaced by a big new one at Hanover Park. I also went to St. Francis School before going to Glynn Academy. The Glynn Academy football team used to play games in a field on Norwich Street.

When Brunswick was laid out, they gave the streets English names like Gloucester and Newcastle, Norwich and Albemarle. There used to be a huge oak tree in Gloucester Street before you got to the Greyhound bus station. Someone wrote a song called "Tie a Yellow Ribbon Round the Ole Oak Tree." That's where it came from. We had a good three or four weeks of nothing but rain, and it just collapsed.

I remember when people used to ride streetcars in Brunswick. They took down a beautiful oak tree in front of our house and put a streetcar on Union. My nurse and my friend's nurse would put us on the streetcar and make the whole round. We used to love doing that. The streetcar went by a men's gun club, where men would go when they got off work and do skeet shooting. The skeet range was right on the marsh near the creek. The men in town loved to go out there in the afternoon and shoot skeet. My husband's father, Vassa Cate, was a champion skeet shooter. They called him "the Boy Wonder" because he never missed. He traveled everywhere. He grew up with Fred Missildine, who taught skeet shooting on Sea Island for years. He also had a son named Vassa, who was a wonderful football player at the University of Georgia.

There was a boat that would go to St. Simons when I was little. It would land at the pier. Our next-door neighbors, the Conoleys, were quite wealthy, and they owned a place right on the beach. He was with the Downing Company. When they'd go to spend the summer over there, they'd take chickens and a cow and a horse with them. They'd go on a barge sort of thing. There were lots of cottages on the beach back then called "the Waycross Colony." They were shanties connected to each other for people who came down for the summer from Waycross.

There used to be a pavilion down at the pier. There was always a lot to do there. I used to take a crab basket and pack a lunch and take the children to the pier to crab and fish. We'd make a day of it and had the best time. Once, we were sitting near the pier eating our lunch, and we could see the water whirling in the sound. Someone said, "This is a storm!" So we got under an oak tree and waited until it was over. I remember a roof blew off of a building. It was right exciting.

This was before the causeway between Brunswick and St. Simons was built. I was there for the dedication of the causeway. I was in a pageant as a little Indian. It was a big event. The architect was Fernando Torras. I grew up with his sisters. He went to Georgia Tech. He was a smart, nice man. He was Spanish. Every now and then, he'd go back to Spain. Everyone said it was a waste of money, and it was impossible to build a causeway with so much water and marsh, but he did.

Eleanor Stiles Cate, 2007

Frances Burns was in a photograph at the dedication. She's related to us. She was a Postell. Her ancestor married one of my ancestors. The reason we moved from St. Simons to Brunswick was because after the Civil War, our family was broke. But the Postells stayed over there [see the Allen Augustine Burns, Jr., narrative].

I remember the first car I rode in. Father got it for Mother. I think it was a Ford. It had green flaps instead of windows. The first car I drove was a Ford. My sister taught me how to drive on the south end of town. The first airplane I rode in was on St. Simons. They were taking people up to circle around for five dollars. It was exciting, of course.

I remember when Windsor Park, which is now a neighborhood,

was a golf course. I always thought it was a shame they took down so many beautiful oak trees. Once, a friend of mine and I had a double date. We were going to a dance on St. Simons, and my friend's date stopped the car in Windsor Park and said, "Who wants a drink of whiskey?" We all said we didn't want one, but he said he did. So he got out of the car and disappeared. Doris said, "A. C., where are you?" He replied, "In the ground!" He had stepped in a huge hole from where they had taken up a tree.

I was on the beach at Sea Island when Paul Redfern flew to Brazil. I was high-school age then. It was a clear day, and loads of people were there. Mr. [Howard] Coffin had just bought Sea Island and wanted publicity. He wanted to get the name out. He was a smart man. It was sad, really, because I think very few people thought Redfern had a chance. Of course, poor thing, the flight was not a success, but it did get a lot of attention.

My family owned what is now Sea Island at one time. They raised cows on it. My grandmother sold the island after the Civil War for five hundred dollars. They were desperate and needed the money.

Brunswick was a little town when Sea Island built the Cloister back in the 1930s. They had a big pavilion on the beach. People who had babies would go over there to dance with the baby asleep in the car. Every now and then, one of them would go out to make sure the baby was all right—unheard of nowadays.

My husband, Henry, was in the navy during World War II. He should have never gone because we had three children. But he felt like he would be a coward if he didn't go, so he went. He was stationed up around Baltimore. The little town we stayed in reminded me so much of Savannah, with the brick sidewalks and all.

I descend from John Couper of St. Simons Island. We pronounce it "Coop-a." John Couper was my father's great-grandfather. John Couper had a plantation on St. Simons, and his son managed

Altama [Plantation] on the mainland in Glynn County. I think the Alfred Jones family owns it now. They used to hold weddings there. The home is gone. They finally decided the taxes were too much, so they took down the house. The Sea Island Company owns the old Couper property on St. Simons. They own everything around here.

John Couper was very successful with some of the crops he grew. Thomas Jefferson recommended that he grow olive trees. Thomas Jefferson and John Couper corresponded because they were both farmers. The olive trees lived for a good while before there was a terrible freeze, which killed everything.

All the plantation owners hated Fanny Kemble [see the Sadie Marie Jackson Ryals narrative]. But you have to understand, she was an English lady who came over here and saw all the black slaves working, you know. It was understandable what she wrote. My father was proud of the fact that the only person Fanny Kemble spoke well of was Mr. Couper.[1] She said he was a nice gentleman.

My middle name is Stiles. A lot of Stiles lived in Savannah, but a few lived down here. The ones that lived at Altama were smarter than the Coupers down at Cannon's Point, because after the Civil War they moved to Atlanta and ended up being quite well off. My cousin Jimmy Couper was a contemporary of my father. He was raised up at Altama before moving to Atlanta. He'd come and visit us in Brunswick. He was a delightful person. Very charming.

Mother put up with Father's bragging about his family. There was a citation about his grandfather being ambassador, and Father always bragged a little bit about it. Mother used to get so embarrassed. She was so amused because one day a priest came to visit, and Father showed him the citation, which he was so proud of, and the priest said, "That is a coincidence because my ancestor was the vice president at the same time." And so Mother got a big kick over that. He just shut Father up completely. He couldn't think of a thing to say.

My aunt Caroline Couper Lovell wrote *The Golden Isles of Georgia* and *The Light of Other Days*.[2] She also wrote "We Are Seven." Aunt Caroline wrote so many diaries, which I gave away, and it makes me sick to think about it.

James Hamilton Couper was on the [steamship] *Pulaski* when it blew up.[3] He wrote an account of the whole thing. Mrs. Nightingale was going to New York with her little girl, and he said he would look after them. He saved Mrs. Nightingale and her daughter, whom they called "Little Lou."

The Oglethorpe Hotel in Brunswick was a great big lovely place. It was a shame they tore it down. It had a beautiful ballroom with huge mirrors on the walls all around, and when you danced you'd see yourself. There was a cotillion club back then, and every year they had a ball—the event of the year. I went to my first one when I was fifteen or sixteen. Everyone wore their best. You formed lines and circled around. You didn't dance with just one person. You danced with everybody. They used dance cards during my sister's time, before the boys got more bold and just broke in on you. We had loads of fun. My uncle Harry led the cotillion. He was my father's brother-in-law. He was a du Bignon. The du Bignons owned Jekyll Island at one time. We had lots of parties at the Oglethorpe. I tried to dance the Charleston but wasn't too good at it.

Uncle Harry du Bignon's mother wrote about the storm of 1898.[4] We never left town when a hurricane came. The old-timers used to say that St. Simons was fixed in a little cove to where hurricanes don't hit over there as strong as they do other places. They said that for years and years and years. I've got a chart that looks like a Parcheesi board, and you can see where hurricanes would go.

One hurricane that came here, I believe it was Dora [in 1964], we had five or six people who lived on St. Simons, right on the ocean. And they were scared. So they stayed with us. My husband was furious. He hated to have extra people, but he put up with it.

We were up all night with the wind blowing. My son had a new baby. That baby is married now.

I think things are better in Brunswick nowadays, certainly better than it was for a while. I tell you one thing that is a big change. We have so many Mexicans here now. It's wonderful for them because they were so poor in Mexico. They got them here to peel shrimp and do things like that. My grandson is a landscape architect with Sea Island. I don't know how many are working over there. He said they're so glad to have the money. In fact, I've seen them in the post office with their checks to send money back to Mexico to their parents or grandparents. It certainly has been a benefit for the area, too.

There is a Cate Road in Brunswick, named after my family. Dr. Cate had a farm on the outskirts of town. They had to sell it during the Depression. When he died, he was still furious that he couldn't have owned it. It's out by Canal Road. James Hamilton Couper was in charge of building a canal that ran across Brunswick. It was dug with slave labor and Irishmen. The Irish were worse off than the slaves were.

I remember when World War I was over because they flew an airplane over the house. I'd never seen one. I was six or seven years old. The people next door took me in their car down to city hall to see them hang the Kaiser. It was just a stuffed thing. I remember that vividly. They put the apparently dead person in a coffin and drove off in a hearse.

A lot of my ancestors are buried at Christ Church. The Coupers especially. Christ Church has a beautiful stained window of the Wyllys and the Coupers. I remember my uncle Charlie Spalding Wylly, my father's uncle. He married my father's aunt. Uncle Charlie's mother was a Spalding over on Sapelo Island. He was a Confederate veteran. When he died, we went to St. Simons on a boat, either the *Emmeline* or the *Hessie*, which ran during the summertime. This was before the highway was put in across the marsh. I was about nine or ten years old. We landed at the town of Frederica on St. Simons. A black man in a horse and a wagon was waiting for the casket. We walked on a dirt road from Frederica to Christ Church. At the funeral, there were poor, pitiful Confederate veterans. Miserable, poor things, you know.

The Taylor and the Stevens families lived at Frederica then [see the Sarah "Sally" Elizabeth Taylor Jones and Dr. Charles E. Pearson narrative]. They didn't want to leave, but the government took it over and made it into a national park.

William Henry Stiles was my father's grandfather. He was sent to Austria as the ambassador. I've got several pieces in my parlor that came from there. One is a huge looking glass with a marble-top table beneath it. You can't see in it now. There are also two chairs. I've got five children, and they know who all of it belongs to. I guess when I die, there's going to be some moving of furniture!

I'm the luckiest old lady in the world. I've got five children, and four of them live here. The one who doesn't has decided to move back from Atlanta.

I was at the Juliette Gordon Low Museum in Savannah recently, and I thought I was in my parlor because I had so many of the same things that are in that museum. Andrew Low was an Englishman, and he married Mary Couper Stiles. Andrew Low was quite wealthy, and he had three children, who were blood kin to my father's people. Her son, William Mackay Low, married Juliette Gordon, who started the Girl Scouts of America.

My family had a plantation outside of Cartersville, Georgia, at a house called Etowah Cliffs. One time, Andrew Low and his family came over from England and visited my father's house there and brought their white maids with them, which was quite a shock to everybody. Over the years, my aunts traveled a lot in Europe and always kept up with the Lows. In fact, there are a lot of Stiles in Bermuda.

Etowah Cliffs was right on the river. It was really pretty. There were two brothers, and each had about seven children. So the aunts finally couldn't stand it any longer and built another big house, called Malborne, about half a mile on the property. We went by train up to Atlanta and then to the homes at Malborne. There was a river there we'd go to. My father said all the boys had their special places where they'd go swimming naked. Grandfather and his wife, seven children, and two aunts, the Mackays, moved there. The aunts were quite wealthy. They sent my aunts to nice boarding schools up north. They loved my grandfather, and they wanted him to change his name from Stiles to Mackay, and said they would leave him all of their money if he would, but he wouldn't do it. He loved his father and just wouldn't. My grandson is Mackay Cate.

Malborne was a noted miniature artist who lived in Vermont. He was known all over the world. He was a first cousin to Robert Mackay from Savannah. Malborne died and left everything to Robert, so he got on the boat and got to New York and got sick and died. He's buried in a cemetery right downtown on the edge of Central Park.

I don't know if they are the same Mackays that came over with Oglethorpe, but it's likely. Some of them were silversmiths. The Mackays were Scotch. In Augusta, there is a big museum that used to be the Mackay trading post. I think Governor [Carl E.] Sanders made it into a museum.

NOTES

1. Frances Anne Kemble, *Journal of a Residence on a Georgian Plantation in 1838–1839* (1863; reprint, Athens: University of Georgia Press, 1984),

265–66. Kemble wrote, "I promised to tell you of my visit to my neighbor Mr. C[ouper], which pleased and interested me very much. He is an old Glasgow man, who has been settled here many years. . . . Mr. C[ouper]'s house is a roomy, comfortable, handsomely laid-out mansion, to which he received me with very cordial kindness, and where I spent a very pleasant morning. . . . Old Mr. C[ouper] spoke with extreme kindness of his own people, and had evidently bestowed much humane and benevolent pains upon endeavors to better their condition." Caroline Couper Lovell, *The Golden Isles of Georgia* (Boston: Little, Brown and Company, 1933), 271. According to Lovell's account, "James Couper could write in 1912: 'Whilst belonging to the class of slave owners, and a Confederate soldier, I say, without hesitation, that no greater benefit ever befell any country than the emancipation of the Negroes in the South. . . . It is true that a civilized people should have found another solution for the removal of slavery, besides war, but the Fire-Eaters of the South and the Abolitionists of the North, the latter aided by such women as Mrs. Stowe and Fanny Kemble, women of marked talent, are responsible for the misery and suffering incurred in its solution.'"

2. Caroline Couper Lovell, *The Light of Other Days* (Macon, Ga.: Mercer University Press, 1995).

3. The steam packet *Pulaski*, under Captain Dubois, left Charleston for Baltimore on June 14, 1838, with a crew of thirty-seven and approximately 150 passengers, of whom about fifty were women. The engine-room boiler exploded about eleven o'clock that evening thirty miles off the North Carolina coast. James Hamilton Couper manned one of three lifeboats that escaped the sinking vessel. His yawl carried twelve people, including several women and children traveling with him, "a Negro waiter," and "two Negro women." Carolyn Couper Lovell's *The Golden Isles of Georgia* recounts the sinking of the *Pulaski* as told by James Hamilton Couper.

4. Excerpts from a family letter in the possession of Eleanor Stiles Cate:

> Tuesday Night, October 4, 1898, Brunswick, Georgia:
>
> My darling May,
>
> I could never describe to you the terror and suffering of last Sunday night. . . . About nine o'clock . . . Aunt Mamie went to go in the room for something, and . . . she saw the side of the house open

and shut. . . . When the next gust came the wall opened about 5 inches and closed, oh, how terror stricken we were. . . . About half past eleven . . . the wind and rain lulled. . . . Fanny Nightingale and I walked over to Leila's, and the water had already risen to the top of the Piazza at Dr. Hazlehurst's house. . . . We looked down Union St., and from the Butts' house straight down beyond the Symons was a flowing river. . . . Capt. Tapper's beautiful home and all those around there had water four and five foot deep.

Carolyn Evangeline Whitfield and Bernice Wilma Myers, 2005, holding a portrait of their grandfather, Ben Sullivan

Carolyn Evangeline Whitfield
and Bernice Wilma Myers

Sisters Carolyn Whitfield and Bernice Myers are the granddaughters of Ben Sullivan, a well-known and highly respected islander featured in several books about St. Simons. Ben was the grandson of Old Tom (also called Bilalli or Sali-bul-Ali), a Mohammedan who was given free rein to conduct plantation affairs in John Couper's absence.

In this narrative, the sisters prove that a well-rounded education can be found anywhere, including a one-room schoolhouse on a barrier island. In reading their recollections, one gets a clear picture of community among the residents of Harrington, located at about the midsection of St. Simons. The desire for education and a strong work ethic that their ancestors possessed was handed down to them and through them to their children.

31

Both Carolyn and Bernice moved to New York City, a common trend at the time, but eventually returned to their roots. They recall the days when islanders could barter for goods (seafood for clothes), when church was an all-day affair, when the older folks still believed in evil spirits (haints), and when many families raised their own vegetables and kept hogs and chickens.

Carolyn: I was born on St. Simons Island, January 31, 1940.

Bernice: I was born March 26, 1943, in Harrington at home. I think my grandmother Carrie and Dr. Chapman delivered me.

Carolyn: Our grandmother was a midwife. She delivered many babies. I was born in the house that Ben Sullivan and my grandmother Caroline Lee Sullivan lived in. He passed away in 1950. He could trace his roots back to Africa, around Sierra Leone.[1]

St. Simons was *really* an island then. Coming to Brunswick meant going to the mainland. Someone would have a car, and we'd come over to Brunswick to buy groceries—what we called staple things that we didn't have at home. We had a lot of meat because we'd kill hogs, and we had chickens. But we would buy flour in Brunswick. They called bread "light bread." The island prices were always for tourists. We went to the A&P on the waterfront on Bay Street in Brunswick at the very end of Gloucester Avenue. My mother used to give me a list and a ten-dollar bill. I was to come to Brunswick to buy exactly what was on that list. I did it.

Bernice: Everybody from the area shopped there—Darien, Brookman. It was where everybody could get together, like a mall. You could buy in bulk, get sacks of flour, grits, and sugar. Later on, we started shopping at Andrews Grocery Store at Glynn Haven [on St. Simons].

Carolyn: Because we could get an account. That was good for the community. And we traded out. We would give them seafood, and they would give us clothes. Plus, my grandmother had holly trees for Christmas, and they would come and get the trees and trade out.

I remember as a little girl that my grandparents had a mill, and they would grind the corn and make hominy. They had little outhouses, and we'd call them names. This one house was where we would keep corn. We would put corn in a grinder, and it would grind up the corn to a certain coarseness. It never got as small as the grain we'd buy in a store, so we called it hominy grits because it was coarser. We grew our own corn and potatoes and raised chickens. My grandmother believed in us being in the yard. We had a number of fruit trees. I saw bananas grow; we had tangerines; we had grapefruits, grapes, oranges, persimmon.

Bernice: Lemon trees.

Carolyn: We had all of them. They were in the Harrington area of St. Simons near cousin Alfonzo's place [Alfonzo Ramsey's Plantation Supper Club]. That was part of the property where my grandparents were.

We saw rice grow. My grandmother kept an area watered, and she would show us how rice grows.

Bernice: She used a hand pump and carried the water to the rice area.

Carolyn: We called that soil "black." It was so rich. They had what they called a pond. From digging that dirt, they'd leave a hole there, so water would fill. I could remember also cotton. I could remember the fuzz. Big Papa called Grandmother "Bama." I guess we couldn't say "Big Mama," so we said "Bama." But he liked it.

Bernice: She would have not a whole field but an area, just two or three rows. She would say, "This is what cotton looks like." She would grow it just so we could see.

Carolyn: Our grandmother worked for the Gould family, a white family [see the James Dunn Gould III and Mary Frances Cannon Gould narrative].

Bernice: She used to travel with them. They sent her to school. She would say, "We went abroad to England and Europe." She used to bring back little ornaments, like of Queen Elizabeth. I think while she was overseas, she took a course in midwiving.

Carolyn: She could have been an apprentice to learn how it was done. Our mother was Katy Sullivan, Ben's daughter. She married someone from the Brookman area named Burnette Rooks.

Bernice: Brookman is out on the highway going to Waycross.

Carolyn: Dad—I called my uncle Cusie Sullivan, my mother's brother, "Dad" because my father passed away in 1945. Ben and Carrie Sullivan had ten children. They had five boys and five girls. They had two sets of twins. Uncle Cusie was a twin. He owned Cusie's Fishing Camp. Years ago, when Ben and my grandmother and Cusie were in their prime, they had a business. People would come in from Atlanta, and they would take them fishing and marsh-hen hunting.

Bernice: They had sort of like a bed-and-breakfast right there at the campsite. I remember my mother used to go and dress up in a uniform and cook. Once the people went out and caught the fish and come back, they would fix it for them right there. And they would spend the night. Ben started it off. The family helped. My mother and my uncle all ran the business.

Carolyn: When Big Papa, Ben, became disabled, then Cusie kept it up. Big Papa died about 1950. He used to call me Carrie. He would say, "Come here, Carrie." I would go sit on his knee. He would be drinking coffee—black with sugar in it. Because it was on a wooden stove, it was hot. He only gave me a little of it. That was like a love thing. I was very thin—skinny. Everybody was trying to fatten me up. Children weren't supposed to drink coffee, so you can remember what you're not supposed to have. I don't drink coffee now.

Bernice: Certain things they didn't want you to know about. If a child was about to be born in the house, they'd say, "Go outside and play." Certain things we weren't supposed to see. They kept that away from us.

Carolyn: We used to hear stories about conjuring. I remember our grandmother used to tell us that she thought there were animals at the foot of her bed and would choke her. We thought she had thyroid problems. Another lady who lived across the street, each night would cut that house up because she thought something was choking her. She would have a butcher knife. When she fell asleep, she would feel the choking and think someone was doing it. So she just used a knife. She believed it was a haint coming to visit her. She would keep these knives. When she was over at her niece's house, you could see her doing this in her chair [waving a knife around her head], like something is coming around her.

I remember my grandmother nailing a penny in the doorstep to bring prosperity. As often as you walked over it, you would attract money. Some people in the neighborhood put a horseshoe over the door.

Bernice: They used to wear heavy clothes all the time. Even in the summer, to protect them from the sun, from the heat.

Carolyn: One layer was to get the sweat. My grandfather, I remember, he was your complexion [white] on his chest.

Bernice: We never had a lot of colds. After Christmas, our grandmother used to give us castor oil. You lined up—everybody.

Carolyn: Cleaned us out! Cleansed us every year. That castor would be either in coffee or juice. If you spit it up, you would take some more. That cleansed your system.

Bernice: Cleaned out all the junk you ate year-round.

Carolyn: My grandmama, because she was a midwife, also had an inkling about how to heal. I knew she had high blood pressure. There was a time when she would eat nothing but rice and water. If you think about it, there was no salt. She knew a lot of ways to heal. We had family that would come from Savannah particularly to eat because she would throw a feast. It took awhile to come down here, but they didn't mind. We always had enough food. Always.

Bernice: If anyone had a problem, they would come for her. I remember when I was little, this man had a problem with his horse. It was constipated, so he came to get my grandmother. She put something together. They got the horse back on his feet and cured him just like that.

But my grandmother didn't like for them to take pictures of her. She was thinking people would make fun of her. Once, she was in the field, and during this time people used to come around St. Simons taking pictures. And she said to this one photographer, "Don't take my picture. I don't want you to take my picture." So he put his tripod camera there, and she took the hoe and chased him out of the field. But I think he did take it because he mailed it back on a postcard. I don't know what happened to that postcard. She probably tore it up.

Carolyn: They believed in festivities because for the holidays they had all that food cooked up. They had an outer smokehouse full of meats.

Bernice: If somebody killed a hog, everybody would come over and help that person clean and dress it, and they'd get a share of it. Someone else kill a hog, and everyone would go over and do the same thing.

Carolyn: My grandmother was a member of Christ Church [Episcopal] by Fort Frederica. The reason she left is because they were telling her where she had to sit. I don't know where they had to sit, but it wasn't as free. She told them, "If you tell me where to sit, I have to leave." Onnie, my grandmother's niece, kept it up and went to the [St. Ignatius] Episcopal church in Jewtown. We went to the [First African] Baptist church. My grandmother became a member there. I remember as a kid we'd go to church all day long. She'd have fruits and crackers and cookies to feed us so we wouldn't make a lot of noise. You would walk to church, about a mile. Ben Sullivan was Mohammedan. He descends from Bilalli [Sali-bul-Ali]. Bilalli, I understand, was brought over as a slave at the age of fourteen.[2]

I don't remember Obligation Pond. That was before my time. Someone much older can tell you about it. Maybe they were using it during their time. I went down to the far end of Harrington Road to be baptized. When that tide was low, we went in. The ministers kept up with the tides. People knew when you had certain things [ailments] in your body or when you were having a baby. They knew that because of the moon and the water.

Bernice: Church was all day. It started out in the morning, and you didn't leave until the afternoon. They had services, and then they'd break because they had covered dishes. Then you go back to night service. Years ago, when a person died, they used to have the body in the house overnight for a few days, and someone would sit up with it. When I was a little girl, I was afraid to go in the front room because there was a body in there.

Carolyn: It was Big Papa, Ben Sullivan. That house is still standing.

Bernice: They laid the body out in a coffin. That's what they did years ago. They were taken to the funeral home in Brunswick, and the body was prepared. Then they brought the body back to the house.

Carolyn: Ben's body is buried at the village [German Village] cemetery on St. Simons. There were five of us in our family. Winfred passed away in October 2002. He was in the navy and then an adjuster for Allstate. Emory still lives on St. Simons. Joann lives in New York. When we were small, we all stayed in the same bed. A standard-sized bed. We went to Harrington Elementary School right here in Harrington. Mr. Adrian Johnson and his wife, Luetta Johnson, were the directors for that school. She had a master's degree from Carolina [Claflin University in Orangeburg, South Carolina]. She was very knowledgeable in a lot of things. They lived in another section of the island. She played the piano at church services, so our parents knew exactly what we were doing. We couldn't hide anything. They knew us. They knew everything about us and taught us well. It was through the seventh grade. School hours were eight to three. Mrs. Johnson taught half of the grade. Mr. Johnson had half of the grade. They had a partition in the middle of the room, and the grades were lined up. There would be the fourth grade in this section, the fifth grade here, and the sixth grade here, and seventh over here. While the fourth grade was doing math, maybe the seventh grade could be doing social studies. We had morning devotion on Fridays.

Bernice: She would have you come up to learn how to read. She did it individually. You'd sit in a row, and everyone would come up and take a chance reading out of this reader, a little reader, *Dick and Jane*. And the ones you missed, she would underline it. The next time, you had to repeat it. Everyone had to come to her desk and read *Dick and Jane* and *Spot and Sally*. There was no talking or throwing things. You'd sit still and do your writing or whatever, and when it was your turn to come up to her desk, you start reading. When you finished, the next person would come up. We had to learn the Bible. We had to learn a Bible verse. If you didn't, you had to go outside until you learned it and then come back in.

Carolyn: When I graduated, there were seven of us. There were forty or fifty kids in the school. By the time I left there and came over to the Brunswick school, I didn't open a book until tenth grade. We were well prepared.

Bernice: Because we were all in the same room. So what the upper grade was learning, the lower grade was hearing it, too. When we got there at that point, we knew what it was all about. We were in the same room, just a different section.

Carolyn: But you had to be a child who would retain it. Everybody didn't retain it at the same rate. We were there from preschool through seventh. We had proms. I could remember a dress I had. It was long. We were chaperoned by our parents, and it was nice. We had to learn the dances and how to waltz. They did a lot of training for us. We didn't realize it, but we thought we were being hampered.

Bernice: We had to put on plays and learn different lines.

Carolyn: I could remember speaking three or four hundred times in plays. No one on the outside but Mr. Johnson would have the book. Most of us had to remember those lines. We'd start three months ahead of time.

Bernice: Our mother would help us read the parts.

Carolyn: If there was schoolwork she didn't understand, she would find somebody who understood it and made sure we got it.

Bernice: I could do the math. Every summer, we used to go to a lady in the community and have math. She found somebody who could teach me how to do math.

At recess, we would play hopscotch and ring-around-the-roses. And you had to do your chores when you got home. They used to have a penny club for picnics at the end of the school year. You would bring your money in to save up for a picnic at Seldon Park [in Brunswick]. They would furnish the drinks and turn the ice cream, and you would bring a sandwich.

Carolyn: We used to have Easter egg hunts on the opposite side of the road from the stables on Frederica Road [at the Sea Island Causeway intersection]. And we would walk down there.

Bernice: We used to go down to Cusie's Fish Camp and crab. And we used to go into the woods and get the wild fox grape to get the plums. We'd get down to the river, sit in the boat, and eat crabs and plums.

Carolyn: We had a strong sense of community. Kids would get together in each other's homes.

Bernice: But before you could do any of that, you had your chores to do. You had to feed the chickens, get the wood in, or pick the corn, iron. On washday, we had to help out because my grandmother took in washing. It was a family thing. You couldn't play around because everything on the line was white. White sheets, white shirts. That was on a Wednesday, when the people brought their laundry. They used to come back on Friday to pick them up. They would come with a big basket, and you had to have it ready for them.

Carolyn: At school, we had little parties. To make a little money, we would sell franks. We used to go in the woods and get palmetto sticks and push the hot dog right through and roast it over a fire. Those were good times. As children, you don't realize what you have until it's gone. And we had a good childhood.

Bernice: Boyfriends didn't come until high school, when we came over to Risley.

Carolyn: We went to Risley in Brunswick on Albany Street. We rode the school bus to Brunswick each day. Our bus driver was Mr. Charlton Scott. He lived on St. Simons. He would have the bus at his place every day. We were the first on the stop and would go all over the island picking up the minorities.

Bernice: Our mother used to work at the Casino [an entertainment center on St. Simons, torn down in 2003, that included a swimming pool, bowling alley, and skating rink]. We didn't go there because it wasn't integrated at that time. We couldn't go there. I used to help her sometimes. When the kids would go in swimming, she used to take their clothes and give them a key to a locker.

Carolyn: We went to see movies in Brunswick on Albany Street. Also, they had a drive-in theater on the island my aunt used to take us to. It's amazing about trust. You knew certain things you were to do and not do. Our parents entrusted you with a lot of things.

Bernice: If anyone saw you doing something wrong, they would say, "You shouldn't be doing that," or "Your parents wouldn't want you to do that."

Carolyn: And I don't remember them talking to us that much about things doing with motherhood. I guess it's how they presented it to us. We knew that there was a time for marriage, and that we wanted to go to school, and we wanted to finish. We had some kind of goal set. We met a lot of people. My grandmother especially was very well liked, so we had a lot of folks in our home. And it made you feel like you want to go up to California even if you never have. "Ooh, no, I'm not going to stay here. I'm going to go to California." You had those inklings that you wanted to get away from home. You wanted to move on.

Bernice: And they talked to you about being something—making something out of your life. Being somebody. And the people you be with. "Watch the people you be with, because people will class you by the people you be with." They told us certain people you don't be with. You don't be with this one. You don't be with that one. Especially girls who are pregnant and unmarried, you can't be with them. No, no. During that time, you couldn't go to church if you were unmarried and pregnant. They were strict during that time. She would be at her home, but you couldn't mingle with her because they considered her a bad girl. To go back to church, I think she had to go to a mother [female elder] of the church for lessons to teach her how to be a Christian.

I went to New York right out of high school to find a job. I did a little factory work in the beginning. I always had to carry my birth certificate around with me because they said, "Oh, no, you're not that age." And I took my diploma, and they said, "Oh, no. This is not a good diploma." That was back in the '60s, and during that time, if you had a high-school diploma from down here, they were saying it was no good. So I had to go to school again. I had to get another high-school diploma. I got into a program where I could work and go to school at the same time. So I went and got the high-school diploma during the day and worked in the afternoon. I don't think high school was any harder up there. I just wanted to make it, regardless. College was a little hard, but I managed to get through that. I went to Bronx Community College and Manhattan Community College. Then I went to Fairleigh Dickinson University in Rutherford, New Jersey. I got my degree in social work.

I got married in '63. When I first went to New York, I was living with my cousin. She was a Sullivan, and she had an apartment. During that time, I was going with a boyfriend I met here at Risley. He went into the military, and I was going to go into the military, too, but they talked me out of it. I wanted to get away and see the world. My cousin said to me, "You know, you can go to New York. They got a lot of training you can get into." I told my mother, "I think I'm going to go there." She didn't really want me to go, but she wasn't going to hold me back. I was really surprised by people who lived up there who didn't know what I knew. I think it was an advantage to me, being from both the North and the South.

Carolyn: I went to college at Savannah State in elementary education. Then I moved up to New York. I went up there because Bernice was there. Like Bernice, I wanted to further my education and went to Hunter Graduate School in New York. When I presented my course of studies, they said I didn't have to take anything. I was shocked. But then, Bernice went a little earlier than I. I liked New York in a lot of ways. In the South, we didn't realize that we were poor. We knew there were some things we didn't have, but we survived because we worked together, we sacrificed, and we got those things. Then, when I got to New York, they said, "Oh, you're from the ghetto, and you're poor." I was a children's counselor and lived in Manhattan. There were a lot of opportunities up there. If you had funds, some days you could just travel if you had bus fare or plane fare. You could go see and be a part of a lot of things.

Bernice: I lived in the Bronx for a while, and then when we got a raise, we bought a house on Long Island. Then my husband decided he wanted to move back south.

Carolyn: Our family is really business-oriented anyway. We grew up that way without realizing it. When business opportunities came to us, we knew how to accept it.

Bernice: My husband had a paper route in Manhattan. That's how we were able to buy our house on Manhattan, because he would work a regular job and have a paper route in the mornings and on the weekends. So we were able to save enough money to buy a home.

Carolyn: It's interesting how things happen and you're not aware of it. Being young, I didn't think of it. Someone told me years later that Miss Virginia Stevens [see the Sarah "Sally" Elizabeth Taylor Jones and Dr. Charles E. Pearson narrative] asked where I was, because she knew I had gone away and she was looking for me. She had asked another cousin of mine about me. She didn't know that I was trying to go to college, but she would have helped me to go. She and my grandmother were very close.

Bernice: Miss Stevens was a white lady. My grandmother used to do washing for her.

Carolyn: The next thing I heard, she had passed. But I would have loved to talk to her.

Bernice: We moved back south because our husbands wanted to, and for the kids. My daughter is in college in Wichita, Kansas, and my son is working in Atlanta. They both went to high school in New York. My daughter went to Savannah State and Columbus [State University]. Then she got married and moved to Murfreesboro, Tennessee, and got her certificate in gerontology. Now, she's in Wichita, Kansas, getting her master's in gerontology. She wants to be a doctor. My son works with a company that puts displays in stores like Kmart.

Carolyn: I have two boys and a girl. The oldest one, David, is in Fort Lauderdale. He works for the department of education, and he also works in the hospital in the evening. He's married, and they have one daughter. Ryan is in Valdosta. He graduated from Valdosta

State. He works for the school as a job developer. He finds jobs for students. He goes and talks to firms about internships for students. His wife works with Georgia Power, and with each promotion, it's a move. He gets jobs as she moves. My daughter works with the gas company. She has three girls. You can go to college to find a career, but at the same time, if you can come out and find your niche, there's nothing wrong with that. We had to let the children know there's nothing wrong with that. Sometimes, college can give you a little preparatory for decisiveness—how to make decisions and have responsibility. Luckily for us, we're doing what our mom and our aunties used to do. We used to think, *What are they talking about in there?* And here we are doing the same thing. We don't realize what good camaraderie this is. We talk about everything.

Bernice: My grandmother used to pay the insurance for everybody in the family—my aunts and everybody. She had this apron, and the apron had these pockets on it. And my aunt used to leave her money, so there was one side for my aunts' money, my uncles' money, my mother's money. The insurance man used to come and sit in this chair, and he had a pocketful of change. And my grandmother would tell us, "Y'all go outside and play. Go on. There's grown-up people talking here." We'd go sit and wait. Soon as he left, we'd dash to that chair because his change would fall out. My grandmother thought, *What's wrong with those kids?* Nobody ever told her we were running to get those coins out.

Carolyn: It was whole-life insurance. She paid nickels and dimes.

Bernice: She was the one who ruled the roost.

Carolyn: Ben Sullivan always wore a white suit and a white hat. He also rode a horse. He looked good in that suit. He never did a lot of talking because our grandmother talked a lot. He was very quiet. He was much older than she was. He could have been twenty or thirty years her senior.

We have property over there on St. Simons and share in paying our taxes. Me, my brother, and Alfonzo Ramsey.

Bernice: People these days really can't afford the taxes. They're so high. A lot of people have a fixed income. A lot of people can't afford to keep it up. And the taxes steadily go up and up, and they have no choice.

Carolyn: Children don't have the same values as we have. They're going to sell their property.

NOTES

1. Orrin Sage Wightman and Margaret Davis Cate, *Early Days of Coastal Georgia* (St. Simons Island, Ga.: Fort Frederica Association, 1955), 155. The authors write, "Ben Sullivan comes from a family that can trace its ancestry back to a definite spot in Africa, being one of the very few Negro families in this country who can do this."

2. Ibid., 153, 155. According to Wightman and Cate,

Ben Sullivan [is] from a well-known St. Simons Island family . . . being the [grandchild] of old Tom, whose African name was Sali-bul-Ali. Tom, who was of the Foulah tribe, was purchased in the Bahama Islands about 1800 by John Couper of Cannon's Point Plantation, St. Simons. Mr. Couper and his son, James Hamilton Couper . . . were high in their praise of Tom's industry, his intelligence, and his honesty. Tom was given positions of trust on the plantation, finally being made the head man of Hopeton Plantation, a position he held for three decades. James Hamilton Couper wrote that he left Tom in charge of the plantation and its 450 Negroes, without an overseer, for months at a time and found him fully capable of managing the estate. Tom, who was a Mohammedan, abstained from the use of spirituous liquors, kept the fasts, and was free of the African belief in evil spirits. He had a Koran and could read but not write Arabic. His African home was on the Niger River, where he was a native of the Town of Kianah in the District of Temourah in the Kingdom of Massina. He said his parents were farmers and were possessed of considerable property. In 1785, when he was fourteen years of age, he was captured and sold into slavery. . . . Sali-bul-Ali had a son who was called Bilalli. After the emancipation . . . Bilalli adopted the family name of Sullivan and his numerous descendants now living on St. Simons . . . own their homes and operate their businesses or follow some trade or profession with the same good judgment and attention to duty which characterized their grandfather.

James Dunn Gould III and Mary Frances Young Gould

Jim Gould is a direct descendant of James Gould, the builder of St. Simons' first lighthouse and the master of Black Banks, a plantation that at one time included Ebo's Landing, the site of a slave mutiny. James Gould and his family were immortalized in Eugenia Price's trilogy of novels—Lighthouse, The Beloved Invader, *and* New Moon Rising.

Jim Gould was born during a period when mule-drawn wagons delivered ice and coal to homes, when the only transportation to the mainland was by boat, and when baptisms of black church members were performed in the ocean at low tide. His narrative provides an interesting study of the interactions between descendants of slaves and masters.

A relative of the Taylor and Stevens families who lived at Frederica, Gould recounts his younger days with both families, when

James Dunn Gould III and Mary Frances Young Gould

he found arrowheads and oyster-shell middens left behind by Indians who hunted and camped on the island. He also recalls the day of Paul Redfern's historic and ill-fated flight from Sea Island to Brazil. His connection with Redfern helped spark Gould's lifelong interest in aviation, which led to his joining the United States Army Air Forces in World War II. He describes an incident during a particular bombing mission in which he almost lost his life.

At the end of Gould's narrative, his wife, Mary Frances, relates an interesting experience of her father's concerning Franklin D. Roosevelt's death in Warm Springs, Georgia, in April 1945.

Jim: I was born February 19, 1922, at my grandfather's home, 1807 Gloucester Street in Brunswick. That is where a shopping center is now located. He owned the whole block from Lee Street to Gordon Street and all the way back to about F Street.

I went to elementary school in Brunswick. It was called Glynn Grammar. There were schools for the colored people on the island then. One was up in Harrington on St. Simons. There was a school for the colored kids on the south end of the island, but I don't remember where it was. The elementary school in Brunswick was next to Glynn Academy. Then you went to the Prep High, then Glynn Academy. Prep was sixth, seventh, and eighth grades. High school was ninth through twelfth grades. The high-school football field was on Norwich Street where the Southern Bell telephone building is now. People would park on both sides of the field, north and south on Norwich Street. In the old days, they had a streetcar line that went out to P Street, where it turned around. My aunt used to chuckle and say, "We're going out to P." I remember the streetcar tracks, but I don't really remember the streetcars.

We had the best football team back then. We won the South

Georgia championship from Macon South in 1939. I played tackle on offense and defense. We only had one team, so you played sixty minutes. We were undefeated. We beat Savannah High, Jesup, Richmond Academy, Benedictine, Waycross, and Albany in the championship game. Old Red Adams was our coach. The assistant coach, Jimmy Sullivan, is still alive. He's in his nineties. He lives in Jesup, Georgia.

My father drove me to high school every morning, and we came back on the bus in the afternoon. There were two buses. You'd pay toll at Terry Creek, the first river on the causeway to St. Simons. The toll was thirty cents for car and driver, ten cents for every additional passenger. And they gave you a ticket. We'd come home from school after playing football, and we'd hitch a ride. In those days, cars had running boards. And so we'd get there, and none of us would have any money. Some folks would say, "Get on the running board." So we'd get on the running board and come up to the toll station. We'd all be hanging on the opposite side of the tollbooth. The driver would pay his thirty cents, and after we'd get down the road a little ways, we'd get in the car. You could usually put two or three on the running board.

When I graduated from Glynn Academy in 1940, Dr. Ward, who was a good friend of ours—he always bought his cars from my father's dealership, Gould Motors in Brunswick—Dr. Ward gave me a graduation present of two and a half gallons of ice cream. Every now and then, I'd help at the soda fountain in the St. Simons village. I'd invite my friends to come in, and we'd dip out of my private stock of vanilla ice cream. That was one of the best graduation gifts I got.

In Brunswick, Glynn Ice and Coal delivered ice in the summer and coal in the winter. They had a bunch of mules pulling those wagons. Well, my father was the Ford dealer and being a good entrepreneur decided they ought to have trucks. So he sold them a bunch of Ford trucks and took in trade mules. I said, "Dad, what did you do with the mules?" He said, "Oh, we sold them hither and yon. Sold every one of them." So he sold them the trucks and also traded for used mules.

The St. Simons property, Black Banks, was given to my grandfather by his mother, Deborah Abbott-Gould, who came over from New Providence in the Bahamas to St. Simons. She married Horace Bunch Gould, who was the son of James Gould—the original—from Massachusetts. Black Banks got its name from the black river mud.

Ebo's Landing was part of my father's land at one time. His father gave it to him. I don't know anything about what went on at Ebo's Landing, other than what I have heard. There were some Africans who refused to be slaves, and when they landed them there at Ebo's Landing, they jumped in the water to go back to Africa. But that was before we owned that property.

James Gould had two sons, James F. Gould and Horace Bunch Gould. James F. Gould married a girl from Connecticut. She didn't like the mosquitoes and all the swampy areas, and she went back north. James F. Gould went to Texas. No one ever heard of him since. My ancestor James Gould, who built the first lighthouse near the village, used tabby from Fort Frederica, probably for the foundation.[1]

When Eugenia Price and Joyce Blackburn first came here, they were looking for the post office and met my aunt, Mary Gould Everett, who was postmistress here forever and ever, amen, until she died. She welcomed them into her house, which was across the street from the lighthouse, where there are now motels. That was Uncle Dutch Everett's house. That's how Eugenia Price got involved with our family. My father had the history of the family. Aunt Mary made a copy of it and gave it to all his brothers and sisters. And she had her copy, which she shared with Eugenia Price. That's how she started on the trilogy novels about St. Simons—*Lighthouse, New*

Moon Rising, and *Beloved Invader*. Every now and then, I'll get a call from someone who's read one of her books. They'll say, "Oh, you're one of the Goulds," and I'll say, "Yes. I'm the remnant."

When my sister, Clara Marie Gould, was a little girl, she and my aunt Messick used to play dolls on that walk-around at the top of the lighthouse. My mother didn't know about that, and when she found out, she almost blew her top.

The lighthouse used to have keepers who lived there. The Hodges lived there, and they had umpteen children. Right next to the lighthouse keeper's cottage was a field, and we used to play touch football there. There were the Hodges, Gerald Lewis, Ralph Everett, Forest Dyal from McRae, Bill Cofer, Ed Cofer, Sam Cofer. All of us used to meet there and play.

Our telephone was a box that hung on the wall. You had to crank the phone box to alert the telephone operator, Miss Davenport. You turned the crank on the side of the box until she'd come on and say, "Number, please." The telephone office was across from the St. Simons Library, next to the Coastal Bank. That house is still standing. An unpaved street runs between the bank and that house. Many a time, I'd call her and say, "Miss Davenport, have you seen my aunt Mary?" who was the postmistress. Miss Davenport would say, "Wait a minute, Jim." And she'd look outside. "Oh, I just saw Mary going down the street." That's how quaint we were.

My father and my uncles used to say steamboats came up Gould's Inlet past Black Banks, going through to Hampton River. The reason it got the name Gould's Inlet is because it fed into Black Banks River, and Black Banks Plantation was owned by the Goulds. My father was in the state senate. He wanted to be sure it would never, ever be called something else. So, back in the 1940s, he made sure it went into the history and maps of St. Simons and that it would always be called Gould's Inlet.

Down at the pier in the village, Dr. C. M. Ward had a drugstore.

This is when Mallory Street was shell, before it was paved. Billy Bacchus had a drugstore. My uncle Dutch had Everett Grocery there on the corner of Butler Avenue and Mallory Street, where Roberta's now is. There was a Woco Pep gas station in the village then. The back of it was a tidal marsh. Steve Parrish, who was Maxfield Parrish's son, built himself a penthouse on top of the garage. It wasn't much—just four walls, a ceiling, and a place for a bed. And he had an axle shaft that hung in front of the garage. During the summertime, every time a good-looking girl in a bathing suit walked by—and the bathing suits then covered much more than they do now—Steve would take a wrench and hit that axle shaft and yell out, "Sweet!" And that axle shaft would make a real resounding noise. Of course, everyone would hear that and run out to see who the babe was that was walking up and down the street. Steve was a very good mechanic. During the war, he moved to Miami and worked for Pan American and was one of their top mechanics.

Right there where the Hogans have their store, Pelican's Perch, used to be the icehouse. We'd buy ice in twenty-five-pound blocks. It would last probably two or three days in our icebox. If you kept the box shut, it may have lasted a week. The cost was probably twenty-five cents per block. My grandmother used to get a fifty-pound block of ice and put half in the icebox. Everything beyond the icehouse was just woods all the way down Ocean Boulevard.

My father grew up here with all of his family. There were four brothers and four sisters. Black Banks covered an area, marsh to marsh, from just south of the Frederica Road and Sea Island Causeway intersection north to Harrington, the neighborhood past the Red Barn Restaurant. That cemetery, about three acres on the east side of Frederica Road just before you get to South Harrington, was given by Horace Bunch Gould to the members of the colored employees at Black Banks after the War Between the States. The folks at the colored church put up the sign because they knew the history of that piece of ground came from Horace Bunch Gould to his former slaves after they were freed, so they'd have a place to be buried. That's why it's called Gould's Cemetery.

A lot of the people in the Harrington area were descendants of the Gould slaves. Ben Sullivan and Cusie Sullivan lived in Harrington [see the Carolyn Evangeline Whitfield and Bernice Wilma Myers narrative]. They were good friends of mine. Ben used to have oyster roasts on the banks of the river, and he'd take out fishing parties. In the fall, the Sullivans would take people marsh-hen hunting—people from Atlanta, Sea Island visitors, from all over.

Frank Hunter [an African-American], whose father, I think, was July Hunter, worked here for my grandfather. The house that used to be in front of this one [2850 Frederica Road] was where my father grew up. It was torn down in 1951. My father built a cottage in 1933 near the King and Prince Hotel. It was the only house built in Glynn County in 1933, mainly because my grandmother's cottage had burned down. She had died in 1928, and Mother inherited the property. And so Dad used the insurance to build a house. It was right on the beach. You go down Arnold Road almost to the beach, hang a left on a little street—I think it's called Downing Street. We lived in the cottage right on the ocean. I grew up there. The blacks would have their baptisms, and they'd come marching and singing down from the church up on Demere Road. The people would be baptized in white. They'd take them down to the beach and baptize them there. That's something that's gone.

July Hunter was a part of the family, so to speak. When they were little boys, Frank Hunter used to come over and play with my father. Frank worked for us after Dad died, but he wouldn't work for us when we lived by the beach. He didn't like that.

When Mary Frances and I first got married, we lived at the cottage by the beach, and I'll never forget that we had large sand dunes out in front of the cottage. One day, some people came by and told my wife, "Mary Frances, do you know the ocean is taking your fence away?" The fence was in front of the cottage by the dunes, and that ocean was eating those dunes out, along with the fence. That was in 1949. Right after that, Dad decided he better put a bulkhead in because he lost three hundred feet of land. The bulkhead was cypress. It's probably still there, underneath the ground. The pile driver was Henry Wilson [an African-American], who worked up at the Frederica Yacht Club and the Red Barn. He also worked for the guy that was building the bulkhead for Dad. And the guy had Henry sit on top of the cypress log. They used a hole to sink the log, and Henry was a big man, and he'd use his weight to help sink it. From then on, he became known as "the Pile Driver."

There were not a lot of people here on St. Simons year-round. When we built this house in 1963, everybody asked me, "Why do you want to build out in the sticks, way out there on Frederica Road?" I told them, "Because my father gave me the lot." It used to be you might see a car every now and then on Frederica Road. I used to walk from our house near the King and Prince to visit my aunt up at Fort Frederica, and maybe two cars might pass. I'd ride with my aunt Berta, who was the affiliate rural mail carrier for St. Simons. We'd make deliveries to the various stops. When the Sears Roebuck catalog came out, the people would be standing by their mailboxes waiting for their catalogs. The rural free delivery area on St. Simons was from about the Sea Island Causeway to the north end of the island.

Dan "Mighty Fine" Cowart from Waycross had a place out on Frederica. He started Glynn Haven. He dug a lake back there. He used to sell lemonade in the summer. He'd take a Coca-Cola bottle and put the lemonade in it with a cork stopper and sell it for a nickel. He did a booming business. That was good lemonade!

But the minute we moved here, Frank Hunter became my gardener. Frank used to bring us clams. He and my wife, Mary

Frances, did a lot of landscaping. Frank was a great, great person. I kept his bank account for him. When he got married, Frank bought his wife a good-looking two-door hardtop—a pretty little car in the 1950s. Frank and his wife didn't see eye to eye. So he told me, "Mr. Jim, it cost me three dollars to marry that woman and the price of a Ford automobile to get rid of her!"

In the old days, my father told me, as you went up Frederica Road towards Christ Church, you could see Sea Island. There were open fields. Sea Island was first called Goat Island. Then it was called Long Island. Then Glynn Island. Longview Shopping Center probably got that name because you could have seen Long Island from there. Longview Shopping Center was originally called

James Dunn Gould III, 2005

Redfern Field or Redfern Airport, named after Paul Redfern, who was from Columbia, South Carolina. That was the first airport in Glynn County. It was located on the west side of Frederica Road where Longview and Redfern Village are now located. It paralleled Frederica Road. The runway ran from southeast to northwest. It was about thirty-five hundred feet long. And that's where I learned to fly. That piece of land that used to be a bank and is now an antique shop is where a rotating beacon stood.

Across the road from Redfern Field on the east side of Frederica Road was a place called Shug's Place. Shug's was where you could go in and get some spirits. They used to taxi the airplanes across Frederica Road because there were a lot of oak trees. They'd put them under the oak trees to get them out of the sun. Later, they built a hangar about where Zachary's Furniture is. That was the beginning of flying in this area. The Taylor brothers—Charlie, Reg, Doug, Archie, all the Taylor boys—owned Redfern Field.

Paul Redfern's airplane was based on Sea Island, which was called Long Island then. They had a big hangar about on Fifth or Sixth Street. Paul was going to fly to Rio de Janeiro in August 1927. Back then, Sea Island Drive was a rutted road. It was a pretty good-sized hangar with planks from the hangar door to the hard beach. He kept his airplane there while he was getting ready for the trip. Lindbergh had crossed the Atlantic in May, so Redfern was hoping to fly to South America from Brunswick. He had a Stinson aircraft painted green with "Port of Brunswick" and "Brunswick to Brazil" on the side of it. To me, it was a very large airplane. There was quite a group of people out there on the beach wishing him well and just wanted to see him take off. I'm sure his aircraft was nothing but a flying gas tank.

My uncle Hunter Hopkins was mayor of Brunswick, and I remember being introduced to Redfern in the day before his flight and shaking his hand. They had just pulled his airplane out of the hangar, and he was going to test it out. The next day, we all watched him take off. I was about six years old. It was a beautiful, clear day. He took off from the north end of Sea Island beach, going south. The first time, he didn't get off the ground. I remember distinctly seeing the tail of the airplane on the back of a Model T truck being pulled back to the north end. And so the second attempt, he got airborne, and that was the last anyone saw of him.

If I'm not mistaken, the Massengale Park property was owned by the Postells [see the Allen Augustine Burns, Jr., narrative]. And Massengale, from Atlanta, built a boardinghouse and four or five cottages there. My grandmother's property adjoined Massengale. When they had a fire that burned Miss Janey Dodd's house, it swept through and burned the other cottages, including my grandmother's. That was the third fire that had come through there. There had been a hotel there called the St. Simons Hotel, which burned. Then they built another one at Massengale. My father was born at the old hotel there on the Massengale property. I've only seen pictures of that hotel. Mother used to tell me that out from the hotel there at Massengale, there was a boardwalk and a big pier with lights on it out there on the beach. Every now and then, when you had a wash, you could see the pilings on that part of the beach. It was interesting to hear them tell how much fun they had on the pier.

Later, the county built the beautiful old Casino down at the pier in the village. It had a big dance floor upstairs, a large veranda all around upstairs. The bottom floor had a bowling alley and sold sandwiches and cold drinks. Rumor has it that one of the boys who set the bowling pins unintentionally set the building on fire. That was a spectacular blaze. That was in 1935.

During my father's time, there was a giant slide at the village pier, which people would use to slide down into the water. That was when the *Emmeline* and the *Hessie* [steamers] used to tie up down at the pier. I barely remember getting on the *Emmeline* and riding to Brunswick and back before the causeway was in use. People used to ride their automobiles on the beach up until after World War II. Right there down by the pier, the county built a ramp. And we'd drive down the ramp and under the pier and ride all the way to East Beach on the beach.

If a hurricane struck, we usually went to my grandmother's house on Gloucester Street in Brunswick and stayed there during the blow.[2]

My aunt Berta, my father's sister, married Captain Doug Taylor [see the Sarah "Sally" Elizabeth Taylor Jones and Dr. Charles E. Pearson narrative]. They lived on the river at Fort Frederica. Doug Taylor lived on the south side of Frederica. Reginald Taylor lived on the north side. Archie Taylor lived there. And the Dodge Home for orphans, which burned down in 1935, was there. If you go across the moat at Fort Frederica, look to your left and you will see three palm trees. In the spring, there are lots of little snowdrop lilies where their yard used to be. That's where my aunt Anna Gould Dodge lived. They used to have the best figs. The Dodge Home boys would sell the figs in the summer for spending money. The Dodge Home was a large, beautiful, old white building where Fort Frederica National Park is. When the government bought all that property where the fort is, they took in with it the Dodge Home and where the Taylor brothers lived.

We used to have family gatherings up at the Taylor brothers' fishing camp on the old Lawrence Plantation. Taylor's Fish Camp. We'd go up on the bank along Mosquito Creek there and find multitudes of arrowheads. And there were oyster banks where the Indians would harvest oysters, eat them, and leave them. On the north end of Little St. Simons, there is another large oyster mound. I imagine the Indians would come down the Altamaha River there to hunt and fish.

Postell Creek, which the East Beach Causeway crosses over, used to feed into the ocean right where the old Coast Guard station is. Before the East Beach Causeway was built, you had to cross Postell Creek at low tide to get to East Beach. They filled that in. My uncle Hunter Hopkins went about damming it up. I can see the mules now, pulling these shovels and taking sand from the beach to fill in that creek. And they had a bulkhead along there. Then they built the road and the bridge and the causeway. That was the beginning of East Beach development by the Bruces, which Bruce Drive is named for. There was Charlie Bruce, Ed Bruce, Robert Bruce, and some sisters. My wife, Mary Frances, knew the sisters. She was in a club with them.

There used to be an Episcopal camp over there on East Beach. And there was a Kiwanis camp for girls on East Beach up until World War II. They were on about Fifth or Sixth Street on the marsh side. After World War II, they shut down both camps. The Episcopal camp was moved down to Camden County. I went to Camp Reese, the Episcopal camp, for several years. It was named for Bishop Reese, the bishop of the diocese of Georgia.

Jim Brown, the great NFL running back, grew up on St. Simons. His grandmother's house sits there where Arnold Road runs into Demere. Right near there on Arnold Road, Willis Proctor had a place called Proctor's Emporium, which was a nightspot for the colored people. It was a jumping place on weekends. Us white teenagers would go down and watch them. Then there were two grocery stores on the island—Uncle Dutch's Store, Everett's Grocery in the village, and Hattie and Joe Follins' on Arnold Road about a block from Demere. They had a gas pump. I used to walk down there with my grandmother to Follins' Grocery to get kerosene for the lanterns in my grandmother's house because St. Simons didn't have electricity back then. Hattie was a very faithful member of St. Ignatius Episcopal Church in Jewtown.

When they filmed *The View from Pompey's Head* in Brunswick, all the cars they used came from my father's dealership on Newcastle Street. The Ford building, Gould Motor Company, was right across the street from the Oglethorpe Hotel, where they were filming. The movie starred Richard Egan and Dana Wynter. So we were all up on the building watching the filming, and Dana Wynter made a U-turn, and I thought she was going to turn the Thunderbird over. Richard Egan was more than a little alarmed. They show it in the movie. My father furnished the convertible they used. My mother and my sister were in the movie. They were in the rocking chairs on the Oglethorpe porch. The movie jumps from the front of the Oglethorpe Hotel up to Factors Walk in Savannah.

The Waycross Colony, which was situated between the lighthouse and what is now the Casino Theatre, consisted of about twenty cottages that ran from the street right down to the beach. They were owned by people who came from Waycross for the summer. I had several friends who used to rent those cottages year-round. One day, one of the cottages caught fire, and they all went up in flames. Right after World War I, in the field from the lighthouse to Mallory Street, the National Guard used to have their summer camp there.

When I graduated, I left here and went to Georgia Tech. One day, on a Sunday, we were playing touch football, the Chi Phis verses the SAEs, and somebody came running down to the field and said, "They bombed Pearl Harbor!" And we said, "Where the hell is Pearl Harbor?" So we all came back to the Chi Phi house and listened to the radio. So a bunch of us went down to the marine recruiting station in Atlanta. We decided we'd be marines. We went inside, and this sergeant looked at us and said, "Boys, go on back to school. If we need you, we'll call you." Disappointed, we all went back. Then we joined the Air Force Reserve as flying aviation cadets. Then they called us up.

I served in World War II and Korea. I was in Italy in the

James Dunn Gould III, 1945

Fifteenth Airborne during World War II. I was in a B-24 serving as engineer and top turret gunner. We flew thirty-five missions. When we first started, they said we had to fly fifty missions. We were losing so many crews, they couldn't keep enough people alive. The life expectancy for most bomber crews was maybe fifteen missions. We flew to Germany, Austria, Vienna. On my thirtieth mission, the Germans didn't like me, and they took it out on me. I moved from the top turret because someone wanted a photographer. And I thought that sounded like it would be interesting. So I went from the top turret to the waist, the middle of the airplane. There were two machine gunners on each side in the waist. And they set up a twenty-four-inch camera, a very large camera, which went down through a camera hatch in the flight deck. We'd set it up so that when we started the bomb run, I could hear the pilot say over the intercom that the bomb bay doors were coming open, and the bombardier would then take charge of the airplane. My job was to take strike photos of the bombs hitting their targets. I'd get pictures of what they called "bombs aweigh." We dropped ten five-hundred-pounders. The camera had what they called an intervalometer. It would take so many exposures over a certain period of time. I used to kid the bombardier and tell him, "You better hit your target because if you miss, I'm taking pictures of what you're supposed to be hitting. I'm going to make an honest man out of you." That's the mission when the flak knocked a hole in the top of the airplane. It came down and hit me. I had just put my steel flak helmet on. If I hadn't done that, they would have had my brains scattered all over the bottom of that airplane.

During takeoff, the engineer was responsible for airborne maintenance while you were in the air. On takeoff, I'd stand between the pilot and copilot. The pilot was busy at the wheel of the aircraft. The copilot was monitoring the instruments and calling out the airspeed. I had my hands on the throttles to be sure they stayed where they were supposed to be—that they didn't drift back. The Fifteenth Fighter Command flew cover for us, along with some of the Tuskegee Airmen. They had P-51s. They had red tails. And there were P-38s.

My wife and I went back to Italy in 1995 to the Adriatic side of Italy. The airfield, San Giovanni [near Cerignola, Italy], is now a wheat field. There were two eight-thousand-foot airstrips. The old group headquarters, which was a castle, is still there. The old briefing hut was still there. It had a sign that read, "Keep your feet off the tables." And they had a little chapel on the base there that is still being used every Sunday. They have plaques in there dedicated to the 455th Bomb Group, the Fifteenth Air Force, and to the memory of the men we lost. They took us to one of the cemeteries with this beautiful marble statue. There were eight thousand men buried there. You look at the names, and I say to myself, "There but for the grace of God lie I." It's very emotional to go there.

During World War II, the navy took on [constructed] McKinnon Airport on St. Simons. The Postells owned that land where the airport is now [see the Allen Augustine Burns, Jr., narrative]. There was an Indian cemetery there, and a lot of the artifacts from that cemetery they sent up to the Smithsonian in Washington, D.C.

St. Simons is pretty now, and it's a nice place to live. But they're putting too many people on it now. Even back then, before we lived on the beach, it was just delightful. We knew everybody, the blacks and the whites. Sea Island has changed. The type of people who used to come there in the 1930s, right after Mr. Coffin developed it and Mr. Alfred Jones took over, they were a different type of people. The crowd now is just different. They're nice people, just different.

The Frederica Yacht Club out by Fort Frederica was a dinner club. They built a dock out there, and they had what they called the *Island Queen*, which was a barge with rooms. This was in the late 1930s. The *Island Queen* was notorious in its day. The ground floor was a bar and lounge. Upstairs were "rooms." They'd take the barge every so often, because folks in those days liked to gamble, and tow it up to Doboy Sound. They'd have speedboats that would run people out to the barge. I asked my father, "What are the rooms for?" And he said, "You don't need to know." There's a picture of the *Island Queen* at the King and Prince Hotel, in the dining room.

Morgan Wynn at first built the King and Prince Club. It was just a small building with a bar and a dance floor. That burned down. So they built a larger one with a beautiful bar, beautiful dining room, beautiful dance floor. And it burned down. And then they built the King and Prince Hotel, a wooden structure. In 1937, it burned down on the Fourth of July. It was one hell of a good fire. People were walking down Arnold Road with whiskey and basins from the hotel. I was on top of our cottage with a hose watering down the roof to protect it from the burning embers. Everyone had a well back then.

I met my wife, Mary Frances, on a blind date. She was born in Atlanta. Her mother was a full-blooded Scotch. Her father was in the casket manufacturing business—the Atlanta Casket Company. You know how automobile dealers have showrooms? Well, I was dating Mary Frances, and her father was going down to the factory and said, "Let me show you my showroom." He went in and flipped on the lights, and there were all these caskets. I said to myself, "This is a slightly different showroom than what I'm used to."

Mary Frances: On the day President [Franklin] Roosevelt died, someone called the funeral home and said he wanted the finest copper deposit casket he could possibly get. Papa went down and got it on the train or ambulance going down to Warm Springs. Papa rode down there with it and was ushered into the bedroom where Mr. Roosevelt was. They had to wait before they could embalm him or move him until Mrs. Roosevelt got there, and she had to come down by train. So they told Papa to help them massage him—his arms and body—to keep rigor mortis from setting in until she got there.

Papa said that when Mrs. Roosevelt arrived and they were standing there, "I looked over on the bureau and saw that famous cigarette holder." He just wanted to have something for a souvenir so bad. But he looked up and there was a Secret Service man looking at him, and he said, "Uh-uh."

NOTES

1. Orrin Sage Wightman and Margaret Davis Cate, *Early Days of Coastal Georgia* (St. Simons Island, Ga.: Fort Frederica Association, 1955), 85. The authors note that "in 1808, a contract was made with James Gould of Massachusetts for the erection of a lighthouse. . . . The lighthouse was in the form of an octagonal tower seventy-five feet high and built of tabby salvaged from the parapets of Fort Frederica and from the abandoned houses of the old fort and town. . . . In 1811 . . . James Gould, the builder, became its first keeper."

2. Abbie Fuller Graham, *Old Mill Days* (Brunswick, Ga.: St. Simons Public Library, Glover Printing Company, 1976). Graham's book contains the following letter describing hurricane conditions on the island:

My dear Sister:

You will be surprised to hear that we had a veritable flood. . . . This Island had been almost submerged. . . . At breakfast . . . water was in the lower parts of the peafield. . . . I ran down to the store room and found the water coming in fast. . . . Going into the dining room . . . windows all burst in and the water up to my waist . . . I made my way to the hall door. . . . The water [was] up to my arm pits. . . . The yard . . . looked liked the ocean, great waves chasing each other across from East to West and striking the trees. . . . Much to our relief the water began falling about 3 o'clock and in an hour after, the danger was passed. . . . All the pretty cottages, bath houses, etc., are piled in one inextricable mass next to the woods. . . . Other families on the Island fared even worse than we did. Some took refuge in trees and were exposed for hours—women and young children—to the dreadful tempest of wind and rain. . . . One man . . . who lived on Egg Island, took refuge on his roof . . . but was soon washed off. . . . He was seen and picked up by the crew of a steamer. He had drifted 60 miles! The exact loss of life among the Negroes will never be known. The rice-fields were swept and they must have been drowned by scores.

Your affectionate Brother [Horace Gould].
October 10th, 1898

LEFT TO RIGHT:
Jacob E. Dart, M. J. Colson, Capt. Charles Spalding Wylly,
John Floyd King, and Neptune Small
COURTESY OF THE COASTAL GEORGIA HISTORICAL SOCIETY

Neptune Small and
Diane Cassandra Palmer Haywood

Diane Haywood is a descendant of Neptune Small, a former "servant" of the King family at Retreat Plantation. Neptune is well known locally, having been featured in books like Old Mill Days, *printed by the St. Simons Public Library, and* Neptune's Honor: A Story of Loyalty and Love, *by Pamela Bauer Mueller. Neptune Park, located between the St. Simons Lighthouse and the village, is named after him and sits on land given to Neptune by the King family.*

Mrs. Haywood, like a number of African-Americans who own land handed down from generation to generation, lives on prime real estate but refuses to sell her inheritance. Her home is situated on former Postell Plantation land across from the Longview Shopping Center. As a child, she counted thirty cars a day driving by her house.

At peak driving times these days, that many cars pass every minute.

The youngest of the narrators in this book, she remembers being baptized in the MacKay River. She also recalls the days before integration, when black island children traveled to a swimming pool on the mainland rather than the nearby Casino pool, which, ironically, was located at Neptune Park, her great-great-grandfather's property.

Mrs. Haywood recounts her church's evolution from a gathering space beneath an oak tree to the current brick structure.

Her family put together an album with stories about Neptune Small, which she shares in this interview. The family's motto is, "We Will Continue the Legacy! We Won't Forget!"

Her words are preceded by her great-great-grandfather's remarkable narrative of the search for his young master's body on the battlefield of Fredericksburg, Virginia, during the Civil War.

Neptune Small: Well, genl'mens, Ise b'longs to de King fambly since my longest 'membrance. I use to sorter had to look after Mas' Butler, Mas' Mallory, Mas' Lord, Mas' Floyd, an' de balance. Well, one day on St. Simons Mas' Butler be token sick, an' 'fore a doctor could come he was dead. Well, Missus she grebe an' grebe an' follow him; I tink de same year de Janneray afore de war. Well, it most brake up de fambly, cos dey was all lovin' peoples. Well, when we heard Fo't Sumpta surrender, all my young masters say we must go; dey don't take advantage of 15 colored peoples to keep out de war. Well, I went wid Mas' Lord, cos when he was a boy he wus mostly wid me.

At fust it wus nothin' but w'en we went to Furginny de truble commence. You kno' I use ter cook fur him and kinder take care of him, cos I wus leetle de oldest. Well, any of you genl'men wot ben in de march from de vally to de place call Fredricksburg mus' kno' wot a time it wer' wen about 25 mile off we could hear de cannon an see de town aburnin'—dat is de lie on de sky. De army marches on tell we cum to whar Mas' Lordy say was Mary Hite. Jus' under de hill I make a fire to cook supper.

W'en supper was reddy I go to call Mas' Lord. He be talkin' to some big officers, an' I wate tell he got thro', an I say, "Supper reddy, young Mars." He cum an eat he supper, but don't talk like mos' de times. W'en he thro' he look in de fire a long time. I ben busy washin' de dishes w'en all a sudden he say, "Neptune, a big fite to-morrow mornin'. Good mens will eat deir las' supper to-nite." It makes me feel kinder lon'some to hyar Mas' Lord talk so, cos he always ben so happy-hearted.

Well, de nex day I see de canon gwine by, an de solders marchin' by, an de gen'rals ridin by, an I know'd trouble wus comin'. Jus' afore 12 o'clock I hyar de canon commence to shoot, den I hyar de muskets begin, den I see de wounded mens goin' ba'k, and den—but, genl'mens, war broke loose on dat day. All day it gwine on, an I keep sayin', "Mas' Lord can't cum, cos de big gen'rals is keepin' him to carry orders." Nite cum, but no Mas' Lord. I stir up de fire to keep he supper warm, but no Mas' Lord. I still hyar de canon an de muskets, an I say to myself, "Dey ain't thro' yet."

Well, after it git good dark I lef' de supper by de fire to go look fur Mas' Lord. I met a officer on a hoss. I ask him if see Mas' Lord. He say not since 2 'clock. I makes no anser, but my heart cum up in my thro't, an I know'd den he mus' be hurt. I gone towards de Confed'rate line wher' dey ben fiten all day, an I ask de officer could I go out an fine my young master. He say, "Who is yer young master?" "Mas' Lord King." De officer say, "I spect you'll fine him out dere, but look out fur de Yankee picket."

I crawl down de hill, ded mens was ev'ry wher' but none look like Mas' Lord. At las' it wus very dark. Den I cum to a officer layin' on he face. Som'body had pull off he rite boot an lef' de lef', cos it wus so bloody. I hyar som'body say, "What yer doin' dar?" I say, "Lookin' fur me young master." He say, "Dat is him." I say to myself, "No, dat ain't my young master," an I gone furder down de line.

Wen I git nearly a quarter mile, I say to myself, "I kno' how I can tell if dat is Mas' Lord." I see my old missus run her han' thro' his hair wen he bin a boy, an she use to say, "My boy, you have such beauterful hair," an I use to feel it myself, cos it wus so nice an curly. I crawl back, an I put my han' on he hair, but de blood wus clot, an de hair didn't feel like Mas' Lord's, but I turn he head over w'ere de blood wus not so tick.

I turn he face up so he could look in old Neptune's face, an I say, "My young master—Mas' Lord, dis is old Neptune. Supper is ready. I ben waitin' fur you. Is you hurt bad?" But he never answer—he, he, he . . . Genl'mens, wait on ol' Neptune a little w'ile. I can't talk now. Genl'mens—he , he, Lord have mercy—he wus ded!

I take him up in my arm. De shells bust an de bullets rattle, but I ain't afraid dem. Mas' Lord, my young master, dey can't hurt him. An ol' Neptune don't care. De nex' day some officers put him in a pine box to go to Richmon'. I say, "Well, when I git to Richmon' dats something else." When I git dere I got de best coffin dey had, an we cum to Savannah an burry him dere. Since den he brothers an sisters bring him to St. Simons at de old Frederica church an burry him w'ere he people restin'. Sometime ol' Neptune, he hair is white an rumatiz is got him, but in de spring time I goes an see dat no cows eat de flowers of'n his grave, an keep de grass from growin' too clos'. Well, genl'mens, I could tell about de Atlanta campane, but I can't tell too much now. Som'how ol' Neptune's eyes ain't strong like dey use to be, an water cum in dem so easy w'en I talk 'bout old St. Simons an my young masters in de good ole days afore de war cum dat token so many good boys away. Good day genl'mens. Good day. Neptune will tell you some mo' sometime.[1]

Diane Haywood: I was born on November 25, 1949, in the hospital in Brunswick and raised here at 1790 Frederica Road. My father, Monroe Benjamin Palmer, Sr., is still living. My mother, Araminta Davis Palmer, died March 28, 1998. My dad worked for [Edwin] Fendig making billboard signs. He put up billboard signs all around the counties—McIntosh, Ware, Wayne. They had to put up rolls of paper. He left there and went to Georgia-Pacific, making sheetrock until he retired.

My mother was a dietitian at Epworth By The Sea [a Methodist conference center located on Gascoigne Bluff] for fifty years. She started working when she got out of school. She never left and kept moving up. First, she made up beds, then became a server, and from being a server to dietitian. When she retired, they gave her a brand-new car for a gift.

When I was growing up, there was very little traffic on the island. You didn't need a traffic light. Now, you get in the turn lane and hope someone will let you in. For fun, growing up, we made up our own games to play. We used to sit and count cars when I was in elementary school. We'd count maybe about twenty or thirty a day. You used to say what color car it was. That was another game we had to play. We couldn't come in and watch TV and play video games all day because there was no such thing.

The north end [the Harrington section] was so far away we saw those kids in church or school. The kids we were around were from South End and Jewtown. Most of the kids came to our house to play. It's a big yard. This part of the island is the highest point on the island. They called it Sugar Hill because there was so much love, and everybody loved to come here and had such a good feeling about it.

Diane Cassandra Palmer Haywood

There used to be a drive-in theater across the road, run by Mr. Stevens [see the Sarah "Sally" Elizabeth Taylor Jones and Dr. Charles E. Pearson narrative]. People started going over to the movies in Brunswick, and there wasn't enough money to keep it running. One day, I looked out the window, and it was burning down. Mr. Stevens used to come over to our house and work on our pump. I used to go over there and pick blackberries. There were just two houses—[the Stevenses' and] the Taylors'—and a field. It's a shopping center now. Longview Shopping Center. They started working on that about the time I got out of elementary school.

When we went to the beach, we'd go to where the Sea Island Golf Course is—right off the golf course. There weren't that many people playing golf then. We didn't go to the pier that much. The pier doesn't even ring a bell with me when I was little because we couldn't go to the Casino swimming pool. We had to go to Seldon Park in Brunswick because of segregation.

I went to Risley Elementary and Risley High School. Jonathan Williams [see the Jonathan Lorenzo Williams narrative] was one of my teachers and my basketball coach. When I was close to graduating, we had maybe four black kids going to Glynn Academy. They said it was kind of hard. That was in 1967. After I graduated from Risley, I went to Spelman College. After college, I came home and started teaching at Risley Elementary. Mrs. Lynn Krauss was the principal. I had been gone for four years, and when I got back, integration had just about smoothed out. I'm sure that first year, about 1970, was a big transition. I taught for thirty-two years in different schools.

I am the fourth-generation grandchild of Neptune Small. There are thirty-five of us still living. Neptune went to the war in 1861. He followed the King boys during the war and took care of them. When one of them was killed, Lordy King, he brought him back to the island. Then he went away with the other brother after that. We put together a family book with some of the stories of Neptune.[2] The album was put together by Arnette Viola Palmer [Mrs. Haywood's sister], Anderlny Palmer Graves [her daughter], Keilier L. Rhodes [her daughter], Creola Barnes Belton [her great-aunt], and me, along with recorded and written notes from the late Araminta Palmer, my mom, and Jasper S. Barnes [her great-uncle]. The book was started in April 1998 and completed in May of 2000, at which time we held the largest Small-Morrison-Barnes family reunion at the Embassy Suites in Brunswick, Georgia, June 29 to July 2, 2000. The reunion was in memory of my mother and Uncle Jasper.

Diane Cassandra Palmer Haywood

All our family is buried there in the cemetery on the Sea Island Golf Course [formerly Retreat Plantation]. It's behind where they have the golf carts. The Sea Island Company keeps it up. That's where Neptune Small is buried. We still have plenty of lots there. I plan to be buried there. I hope so. My mother's there. My grandmother's there. Uncle Jasper Barnes is there. My aunt Creola Belton is there. She was one of the first black nurses at the Brunswick Hospital. She also taught school in Glynn County. Neptune helped plant some of those trees that make up the avenue of oaks going to the Sea Island Golf Club.

Neptune, Sr., was born August 4, 1796, and died before 1853 at Retreat Plantation. He worked as a carpenter at the plantation. His wife, Sukey, was born before 1817 and died June 1, 1852. She was a nurse at the plantation [slave hospital]. Neptune, Jr., was born September 15, 1831. His first wife, Ila, which my mother's sister Ila Davis Williams was named after, was born December 30, 1834. They were married on March 28, 1858. To this union, three children were born—Leanora (my grandmother was named after her), Louturia, and Clementine. Neptune's second wife's name was Charlotte Galing, born 1852, married December 14, 1876. To this union, two children were born—Cornelia and Clarence Small. Neptune remained loyal to the King family until his death by keeping the grave site clean of leaves and rubbish.

Neptune Small's house was between the pier and the lighthouse where the big oak trees and picnic tables are. There's a small monument dedicated to him near there. I'm not sure what happened to that land. Somehow, it got finagled, and the county ended up with it.

We have an original letter published in the *Atlanta Constitution* given to one of Neptune's daughters when he died. It's at my mom's house now, hanging on the wall in a frame. She lives on Demere Road right next to the water tower. We also have a big photograph of

Neptune that takes up a lot of wall space. The frame is heavy. It's in the original frame. It's in black-and-white. I have a family history of the Barnes family, too. One of my grandmother's brothers, George Morrison, worked at the Dodge Mills [lumbermills on Gascoigne Bluff].

George Morrison owned all of this property on Frederica Road from my uncle Jasper's house across from the Atlantic Bank to Hanover Square. Uncle Jasper's house is the only house on the island with a basement, unless they've put some in lately. Mr. Buck Buchanan [see the Gloster Lewis "Buck" Buchanan narrative] helped build that house and dig that basement out. There were lots across the front of Frederica given to each of his children, and it was passed down. We still have two front lots where Uncle Jasper's house is and where my house is. I'm not sure how many acres they go back. They go all the way to the back of Barnes Plantation. When I was coming up, it was where we had a hogpen and the chickens. It was the back part of the property—about where Tennessee Avenue is now, or the backside of that. Somewhere in there.

The Barnes Plantation was named after the heirs—Jasper S. Barnes, Creola Barnes Belton, William Barnes, Sr., Araminta Davis Palmer, and Ila Davis Williams. It was called a plantation because most of the subdivisions on the island are called plantations, after the slavery era of this island in past history. Neptune Small was among the first to be freed from slavery.

Every now and then, people ask us to sell our land. But they get the same answer. Lots of people are selling off their property. We're going to stay right here where we've been all the time. Stay right here. It's home.

Jasper Spencer Barnes was the fifth of eight children of James and Creola Barnes and great-grandson of Neptune Small, Jr. Uncle Jasper served on the Glynn County Water and Sewer Commission and ran for county commissioner. He liked hunting, fishing, realty investments, and attending all family activities. He was known as the godfather of the family. He died Saturday, October 24, 1998, at 5:02 A.M.

Our family is a very closely knit group. What affects one affects all. Our motto is, "We Will Continue the Legacy! We Won't Forget!"

Our church, St. Paul's Missionary Baptist on Demere Road, has a lot of history to it. We used to hold baptisms at the second bridge, MacKay Bridge. That's where I got baptized. We drove to the bridge then. Probably they walked when my mother and aunts were baptized. We have a pool inside our church now. All we have to do is draw the drapes back.

When St. Paul's Baptist first started, they had their first services in an old barn that used to be an airplane hangar at Redfern Field [on the northwest corner of Frederica and Demere roads]. I don't know whose barn it was, but they gave us permission to use it. Before that, the founders of our church used to get in a rowboat and row to Brunswick to go to church. Our church is 129 years old this year. So that was 129 years ago [around 1877]. There were six of them who would row to Brunswick. Some people couldn't go, so they decided that rather than row to Brunswick to go to church on Sunday that they'd find a spot over here on St. Simons. They started having church up under an oak tree, I'm assuming somewhere in the Jewtown area. Then they started using that barn. From there, we built a wooden structure. From the wooden structure, we got the brick building where we are now on Demere Road. Mr. Buchanan and Jasper Barnes helped build that church.

The island now is really commercial. It's overwhelming. Everybody seems to be in a hurry now. They don't seem to take time to do anything. People are not quite as polite as they used to be. Traffic is horrendous. You only try to get out at a certain time of day. We've got it down pat when we want to leave—between nine-thirty and quarter to eleven, or you go out between one-thirty and three-thirty. It's like the city trying to move in, every little nook and corner. Like the city trying to move in and take over.

NOTES

1. From a newspaper article by J. E. Dart, reprinted in Abbie Fuller Graham, *Old Mill Days, St. Simons Mills, Georgia, 1874–1908* (Brunswick, Ga.: St. Simons Public Library, Glover Printing Company, 1976).

2. The following excerpt from the Haywood family album, written by descendants of Neptune Small, is presented courtesy of Diane Palmer Haywood.

> Neptune Small was born 15 September 1831 at Retreat Plantation to parents Neptune Sr. and Sukey. He was immediately chosen as a playmate to the King boys, William Page, Thomas Butler Jr., Henry Lord, Mallery Page, John Floyd, and Richard Cuyler. However, a fast bond soon emerged between Henry Lord "Lordy" and Neptune that could not be broken, even after death.
>
> When hostilities broke out between the states culminating in the Civil War, the King boys were quick to sign up. Lordy joined in 1861, and as was the custom of the aristocratic plantation elite, a body servant accompanied him, Neptune Small. Did Neptune freely volunteer, or was he required to go as part of his indentured service to the King family? After all, Neptune was newly married to Ila, his true love, and she had just given birth to a daughter, Leanora. What man of any stature would want to leave his new family, especially if he didn't have to? Many stories have been written about the . . . account, and some are hard to believe because they are being told by white people whose opinions may be biased on the situation. As was custom, it was more polite to say that everyone was a willing participant in their life, including former slaves. So it is unclear how Neptune really felt about the situation. We do know that the outcome could not be anything other than what it was, no matter what our ideas or beliefs about the institution of slavery. Neptune could have easily come home—alone.

John Spencer Harrison "Harry" Aiken, Jr.

In 1736, James Oglethorpe stationed John Humble, the island's first harbor pilot, on the south end of St. Simons. The property was later granted to John Chubb for his military service in Oglethorpe's Regiment. Chubb sold the land to Thomas Spalding in 1786. After purchasing Sapelo Island, Spalding sold Retreat to Major William Page, a friend of Pierce Butler's. Page's only surviving child, Anna Matilda Page, married Thomas Butler King of Massachusetts. King was a prominent public servant who served in the United States Congress, was an early advocate for a transcontinental railway, championed America's infant navy, and was appointed first collector of the port of San Francisco.

Harry Aiken, Jr., is a direct descendant of Thomas Butler King. Harry contrasts the island life of his ancestors before and after the

Civil War with life on the island when he was growing up in the 1950s and 1960s. He offers insights into a post–Civil War transition point in the 1880s, when islanders like Mallery King and James Postell began to see the area as a tourist destination long before Howard Coffin's arrival in the 1920s. Coffin purchased Retreat, which is now a golf course owned by the Sea Island Company.

The much-photographed avenue of live oak trees at the golf course's entrance once formed the entrance to Retreat Plantation. In Early Days of Coastal Georgia, *Orrin Sage Wightman and Margaret Davis Cate describe the road as "wide enough for carriages. . . . Work such as the building of roads was planned for the seasons when the crops had been gathered and the slaves could be spared from work in the fields. In Georgia, men were required to do roadwork in the militia district in which they resided. . . . Mr. King obtained permission to use the Retreat slaves in building this new road. . . . In 1848, Mrs. King announced that a new road to New Field was being made and that all the field hands had been at work on it. . . . Time, and the relentless hand of man, have spared only [a] short stretch of the century-old oaks of Retreat Avenue."[1]*

Harry describes boat racing during the plantation era, when bets ranged from a cigar to a glass of toddy to a beaver hat to a pair of "Durffee's Best Made Boots." He relates how the village on the south end of St. Simons came into existence and also touches on liquor smuggling during Prohibition.

I was born on December 5, 1949, in Jesup, Georgia. My father, John Spencer Harrison Aiken, was working at the American National Bank in Jesup at that time. My family descends from the Kings of Retreat Plantation on St. Simons. My mother is Laura Pirkle Aiken,

John Spencer Harrison "Harry" Aiken, Jr.

from Atlanta. My grandfather was Isaac Means Aiken. His father was Franklin D. Aiken. Franklin married Florence King, who was Mallery King's daughter. Mallery was Thomas Butler King's son, which makes Thomas my great-great-great-grandfather.

Mallery King, the son of Thomas Butler and Anna Matilda, was an interesting person. He had all kinds of schemes going on all the time. When the plantation days were over, the only thing they could do was harvest lumber. Thomas Butler King was a legislator and was away trying to get the intercontinental railroad going at that time. So he was gone most of the time. But Mallery was here with his three sisters. Mallery worked at the Dodge-Meigs Lumber Mill on Gascoigne Bluff, and at the same time he was trying to save Retreat because it had been parceled off by then. I don't think they had Newfield anymore. They had the heart of the plantation, and he was trying to find a way to save it.

The first thing he tried to do was to make it a resort because they used to have a lot of parties over there. He would advertise that they had rooms for people to stay, for people to come over for a week or whatever. They'd plan beach outings and island tours. This would have been between 1870 and 1883. In 1883, after he didn't have much luck doing that, he leased out Retreat to a gentleman named Mercer, who had established inns and hotels throughout the country. But that didn't work out either. I guess people weren't ready to come and just vacation down here like that. It was still people from Brunswick and Waycross coming over for the summer and leaving for the winter. They used to have a lot of parties at Retreat in what they called Grasshopper Hall. Whether it was an atrium or a special building, I don't know. It's where they had their parties. Each of the children were musically inclined, so they had skits and plays with costumes.[2]

Then Mallery was recruited as the first cashier [manager] for the Brunswick Savings and Trust Bank, which became American

National Bank. During his tenure at the bank, President Grover Cleveland made him the customs officer for the port of Brunswick. He held that office during Cleveland's four-year term.

When he decided that he couldn't make Retreat a resort, he kept the main part of the property, but he subdivided what would become King City into 140 lots. It was the first subdivision on St. Simons. Each lot was forty by eighty feet. Each of the smaller lots were sold for a hundred dollars. If you paid cash, you'd get the lot for eighty dollars. They stretched from Floyd Street to Gould Street on that land between the lighthouse and Retreat. Adjoining Mallory Street, there were forty-by-ninety-foot lots that targeted businesses. Then he also laid a two-hundred-by-two-hundred-foot lot for a hotel. This was around 1890.

I have one of the original posters for King City. It reads, "Ye gentlemen, let the ocean blow through your beard." That kind of thing. By 1895, he sold over a third of the lots, bringing in $3,450. The streets were named after his sisters, brothers, or cousins. Florence, Georgia, Virginia, Lord, Page, Wylly, Frazer. Mallory Street on St. Simons is misspelled. It should be Mallery Street. When he signed his name, he swirled the *e* in his name and make it look like an *o*. His signatures on some of the old bank documents look like *Mallory*.[3]

When he was a commissioner, he was the first to shell the roads with oyster shells [using deposits from Indian middens]. The roads had just been dirt paths. I have an old chart of Retreat Plantation. The avenue of the oaks used to extend pretty far down Frederica Road. I have a letter that Anna Matilda Page King wrote in 1848 where she announced that a road to Newfield was being made and that all the field hands had been working on it. She said it "goes in a direct line from Sukey's house and shortens the distance by about a quarter of a mile." There were plans to have 500 trees, 250 on each side, go the distance. Newfield is where the St. Simons airport now is. The Tabby House [see the Gloster Lewis "Buck" Buchanan narrative], which is the only remaining slave house there, would probably be part of Newfield. So the avenue of oaks went a good deal further than what is there now. I don't know what happened to the rest of the trees. The island used to have a big lumber operation, so that may be what happened to them. Or they could have been cleared out when the airport was built for the navy during World War II.

Retreat Plantation's boundaries probably went from the southwest corner of St. Simons up to where Gascoigne Bluff is, east to the lighthouse, where they gave Neptune his property, and north to where the airport is. Neptune Small's house was probably right there in what is now Neptune Park by the pier [see the Neptune Small and Diane Cassandra Palmer Haywood narrative]. Anywhere in there where the old Casino is or where the Waycross Colony used to be by the lighthouse. There are no markers that show where it was.

I used to run a magazine called *Coastyle*, and I wrote an article on the river dugouts [boats] that planters used to hold races with other plantations. Hampton Plantation was one of the main ones to do it. They were racing back in 1830. I don't think Thomas Butler King ever participated in those races. Pierce Butler was big into the races. They held races up and down the coast as far south as Jacksonville. They bet lots of money on them.[4]

My ancestors, the King family, went to Christ Church, which was quite a haul in those days. During the Civil War, Northern troops pillaged Christ Church and looted the island. One of the things they took was a clock from Retreat. It was later found in an antique shop in Attleboro, Massachusetts, and returned to Retreat and put in what was then the Sea Island Clubhouse. In 1936, the clubhouse burned, so the clock was destroyed with it.

My grandparents used to live by the ocean on Florence Street in a house called Sea Marge. When my father was growing up, their dogs would swim over to Jekyll and play on the beach over there when the channel between St. Simons and Jekyll wasn't so wide. It wasn't that far a swim. They would yell over to the dogs to come home.

When they started dredging the channel between Jekyll and St. Simons, all hell broke loose. A lot of people blame it on Hurricane Dora. I remember playing on the beach down there west of the St. Simons Pier. It was sandy, there were dunes, and the waves were good. Now, it's just rocks and mud.

There were bootleggers down here during Prohibition. They'd fly planes from the Bahamas up here before the Malcolm McKinnon Airport was built and land at the old Redfern strip. They'd land the plane, and the police would be there, and everyone from Sea Island would be there to pick up their liquor.

Growing up on St. Simons, we lived on East Beach in the Hardwick Cottage on Fifth Street. There was a Camp Reed on Fifth Street. Then we moved to the end of Ninth Street, the last house on the left by the beach. I remember going to a party at Colonel Brown's home. It was when people were leaving Cuba because of Fidel Castro. Fernando Brito was there, and he had two sisters or cousins who were really cute. There weren't many houses on East Beach then. Daddy built our house using bricks from the old Oglethorpe Hotel in Brunswick. Lamar Davis did the same thing with his home at Kelvin Grove. All we had in front of us were dunes and ocean view. It was beautiful. Now, there's a house built in front of it, built on what used to be a sand dune. East Beach is the most intelligent subdivision that St. Simons has because they built far enough back. People don't panic if there is some erosion or accretion. But Georgia's speaker of the House is trying to build in that accreted land, too. A lot of the old cottages you used to see on East Beach are gone, and they'll be two-, three-, or four-story homes in their place, which is not in character with the neighborhood. They have a plan for the village, which includes plans for five-story buildings, which is just nuts.

In the winter when I was growing up, you played football, and in the summer you played baseball down at Mallory Park. You'd go to the Island Playhouse and watch the St. Francis girls play basketball every Saturday. The playhouse was like an old-fashioned gymnasium. I took dance lessons from Nancy and Tom Gallagher there. They were the dancers on Sea Island, but they also taught dance. The playhouse had a stage, too, because we used to go to see minstrel shows there. All the families would go. Lord knows, you can't do those shows anymore. And there was a projection room. I think the navy built it for recreation purposes during World War II. Sam Cofer had a club by the pier. I think it was called the Beach Club, a restaurant and bar that was on stilts and extended out over the water. It was really cool.

There used to be a baseball diamond, a practice field, in the open space between the Tabby House on the corner of Frederica and Demere roads and the farmers' market. This was before they lengthened the airport runway. Home plate would have been about where the recycling center is now. A home run would have hit Demere Road. I remember Taylor Adams' father taking me and Taylor and Buddy down there to play catch and hit some balls. I imagine the field was left over from the navy days, too. I had always heard that Mario Cuomo played minor-league ball with the Pirates organization in Brunswick. He played for the Brunswick Pirates. Floyd Faust, a local, played on that team.

There was no Brunswick High at that time, so everyone was at Glynn Academy. You merged with Jane Macon when you got out of Glynn County Junior High, so you made new friends. I don't remember that many blacks going there. They must have been at Risley High. Even though I grew up on St. Simons, it seems like I always dated the girls who went to St. Francis, the Catholic school, because they had the cutest girls.

I was a freshman at Glynn Academy the year they won the state football championship in 1963 or '64. It was one of the few times I remember the whole area pulling together. They had parades and pep rallies that the whole town came to. You had Tash Van Dora, and Tullis, and Mumford. All the big boys. They had been big in sports, and it really clicked that year.

There used to be high-school fraternities and sororities back then. The sororities were the PAMs [Pi Alpha Mu] and the Pirates and maybe one other. We had two fraternities, the Phi Gams [Phi Gamma Alpha] and the SAD [Sigma Alpha Delta] Boys. We called them the SAD Boys because they couldn't be Phi Gams. My first year at Glynn Academy, I was a pledge as a Phi Gam. These were the days when all of the brothers would have a meeting with the pledges, and they'd say, "Grab your ankles." And they had big paddles, and they'd beat the s--- out of you. It was terrifying. I don't know why I even did it, but that was an important thing to do. In school, that was the social deal. You had your parties during the year. Each fraternity had pins for your girlfriend. School mornings, you'd meet on the steps, and it was divided, with the Phi Gams here and the SAD Boys over there. The sorority girls would be floating back and forth between the two.

The pledge thing lasted most of the football season. During games, we had to run and get Cokes for people and do something stupid. I can't remember watching that many games except the championship game. I remember that after the game all the fraternities were getting together because there was a group of navy or marine guys who made trouble for some girl, and we were all going to go find them and beat them up. It was ridiculous.

In the village, you had O'Quinn's Men's Shop where Frederica Station is. And there was Ward's Drugstore [and] Palmer's and Maxwell's five-and-dime stores. Palmer's was closest to the ocean. Before they remodeled Maxwell's, it had wood-slat floors. You walked in and you kind of walked down. It was old and dark before they enlarged it. They had a soda fountain and a glass walk-through door that led to a little restaurant next door.

Mallery King envisioned having a bunch of shops there. At one time, there was a hotel. There's an old picture of the village with a boardwalk and the St. Simons Hotel and buildings in the background.

When I was younger, there wasn't a lot of interaction with blacks on the island. The interaction was with people like our maid, Emily Ramsey. She was one of the original Sea Island singers that Lydia Parrish recorded. Those were the days of the washboard band on the island. They knew all of the old, old songs.

She once told us she had to take some time off to go up to Washington, D.C., for the rally with Martin Luther King. Little did we know she had a twin sister. Both of them were missing their front teeth. She showed up one day with her twin, and it freaked out the whole family because we had no idea, and suddenly there are two Emilys—Emily and Cornelia.

My younger sister, Caroline Aiken, a professional musician, claims Emily is her main inspiration for becoming a musician. Caroline still plays all over Atlanta. She's played backup with Bonnie Raitt, and Bonnie Raitt has played on her CDs. She's like the earth mother of Atlanta.

My family has land up in Hall County near Lake Lanier, which got annexed into Buford. We've had it since a lottery in 1806. About fifteen years ago, we started developing it.

The King sisters deeded King's Park to the county for recreation purposes. Mallory Park is where the baseball fields are on the island. King's Park is across from there on the other side of Mallory Street. They found an Indian burial site in King's Park a number of years ago. The wording in the deed for King's Park states that it is specifically for the use and the entertainment of the white race.

One of the baseball fields is named after Lefty Butler. I remember when he was still coaching Little League baseball. He lived on Butler Avenue, so I guess he was related to the Kings somehow.

The two radio stations people listened to when I was growing up were WMOG, which stood for "The Marshes of Glynn" [immortalized in the Sidney Lanier poem of the same name], and WGIG, "the Golden Isles of Georgia." WGIG is now talk radio. MOG was called "Johnny Reb Radio." I'd call in and make requests. The disc jockey owned a record store in Brunswick.

It's not long before the board of education decides to sell St. Simons Elementary. That's coming, and it's really going to be nasty when it happens. Those huge condos they built by the school just make you sick.

I was one of the cofounders of the Round Table and the St. Simons–Sea Island Coalition. We tried to get St. Simons incorporated because we were tired of having Glynn County commissioners apply the same ordinances everywhere, mainland or on the island, and that just doesn't work. People down here aren't motivated. They don't want to get involved in the local politics. The young kids are just as bad.

St. Simons used to be a really good place growing up. The wealth wasn't as noticeable or as significant. Now, the place seethes with money, and there's less in between.

NOTES

1. Orrin Sage Wightman and Margaret Davis Cate, *Early Days of Coastal Georgia* (St. Simons Island, Ga.: Fort Frederica Association, 1955), 71.

2. A letter to *The Advocate* of Brunswick, Georgia, on June 30, 1883, detailed one such event:

Mr. Editor:

As one of the delighted guests on the occasion, please allow the writer . . . to mention a most enjoyable entertainment at the residence of Captain Mallery P. King, on Friday evening, 22d inst. A fancy dress ball was the order of the evening. . . . The costumes of the ladies exhibited great taste and fidelity to the characters assumed. . . . Below is a list of the ladies, with the characters present: Grandmamma, Miss Abbie Fuller; Patience, Miss May King; The Fish-wife, Miss Mercer; Court Minstrel, Miss Buford King; Dolly Varden, Mrs. Mercer; Red Riding Hood, Miss Flo. King; Spanish Peasant, Miss Angie Gould; Betinna, Miss Emma Postell; Lady Washington, Miss Anna Gould; French Peasant, Miss M. Postell; Girl of the Period, Mrs. Macintire. Dancing was indulged in till near midnight, when supper was announced. . . . Supper over, dancing was resumed, and not until a late (or, rather, early) hour did the merry party disperse, long to remember this thoroughly enjoyable occasion.

3. Edwin H. Ginn, *The First Hundred Years: A History of the American National Bank of Brunswick* (Brunswick, Ga.: Glover Printing Company, 1989), 7. Even in the nineteenth century, newspapers had trouble spelling Mallery correctly, as this passage from Ginn's book illustrates: "On September 1st, 1890, the following newspaper notice appeared: 'Stockholders Meeting—A meeting of stockholders in the Brunswick Savings & Trust Company will be held in the office at 4 P.M. Sept. 30 to consider the advisability of increasing its capital stock to $100,000.—Mallory P. King, Cashier.' "

4. Harry Aiken, "Hampton Racers Sing This Song in a Dugout," *Coastyle* (Spring 1995), 11. Aiken quotes from *Early Days in Coastal Georgia* in describing how "the gentlemen gave fanciful names to their craft—*Comet, Swan, Flea, Lizard, Leopard, Star, Minerva, Sunny South, Goddess of Liberty, Devil's Darning Needle, Lady of the Lake*—and painted them and costumed the crew accordingly. The *Goddess of Liberty*, a six-oared boat, thirty-two feet long and three feet, eleven inches wide, was painted white, with a blue band in which there were twenty-four stars (for the twenty-four states of the Union), while the crew was dressed in red. The *Devil's Darning Needle* was painted black and the crew was dressed in green. The crews, trained to a high degree of perfection, frequently covered the half-mile course in two minutes, twenty seconds." *The Advocate*, May 1831. The

paper quoted Liverpool Hazard as saying, "Old marster was good to his oarsmen. For three months before the race he wouldn't let any of us do any work. He would lock us up if we did. We'd just eat and practice and make our muscles strong. He'd sit on the stern of the boat and would keep urging us on by calling us by name when we would slack up. At our best we could row the mile in six-and-a-quarter minutes. Old marster love the races and would bet $500 every time. When we would win, there'd be some celebrating. Step all night long. Everybody would make a fuss over us. Everyone wanted to be on marster's crew."

Viola Vonceal Abbott

Viola Abbott lives on property that once belonged to Georgia's founder, James Oglethorpe. Mrs. Abbott is related to Carolyn Evangeline Whitfield and Bernice Wilma Myers (see their narrative) through Lavinia Abbott, Ben Sullivan's sister. Her great-grandfather Randolph was a servant of Captain Charles Stevens. Both served in the Confederate army.[1] After the Civil War, Randolph and his brother, Tom, adopted the surname of a family living at Frederica.

Tom Abbott's son, Robert Sengstacke Abbott, achieved fame and wealth as the founder—starting in 1905 with a total capital of twenty-five cents—of the Chicago Defender, *a weekly newspaper that eventually made him a millionaire. Robert Abbott, whom Mrs. Abbott refers to as "R. S." in this narrative, encouraged blacks to move north in support of "the Great Migration." It is estimated that more than a million Southern blacks migrated north between 1915 and 1925.*

During the Depression, Robert Abbott sent money to family and friends back on St. Simons Island, including the Stevens family.

I was born on St. Simons, February 27, 1931. A midwife came in and delivered me. My younger sisters and brothers were hospital babies. My mother had eleven children. I'm right in the middle. The midwife who delivered me came from Brunswick. Carolyn Whitfield's grandmother [Caroline Lee Sullivan] was a midwife. Believe it or not, my mother remembered all of the midwives who helped birth her children, except for mine. For one thing, she used to faint every time she gave birth.

I was born an Abbott. I've never been married. My middle name is Vonceal. You don't find many Vonceals. I don't know where my mother found it. My sister was Mildred Maxine Abbott Atkinson. She died in 1999. She was the historian in the family.

My people, black people as a whole, never have written history. In the first place, people didn't care about them, and then they were so secretive or could not read or write. We had an oral history, and you passed it down from one generation to the next.

The Abbott name came from a slave owner. If you've read Eugenia Price's books, there was a Sally Abbott. She was a slave owner, and of course some slaves took their names from their owners, and I guess that's where the Abbott name came from [see the Sarah "Sally" Elizabeth Taylor Jones and Dr. Charles E. Pearson narrative]. I like to read Eugenia Price's books. I love her books because they have to do with what happened on St. Simons years ago. She and my mother were good friends.

My parents were raised on the island. My mother's name was

Mildred Cuyler Abbott. She was born in Brunswick. My father, Malcolm Lee Abbott, was born on the island. He was a chef at the old Frederica Yacht Club and then at the Red Barn. He was also a carpenter. We had a lot of carpenters in the settlement around here. We had to build our own houses then. He would also lay bricks. His nickname was Jack because he was a jack-of-all-trades.

Frederica Road used to be covered with ground-up oyster shells. We called it "the shell road." I don't remember walking on any paved road or dirt between here and the stables [at the Sea Island Causeway]. I don't know how Obligation Pond [near Harrington] got its name. I wish I knew. When we grew up, everybody around here had a dialect. Just listening to that slave dialect, it was Ab-ee-gation Pond. And I didn't know it was Obligation Pond until I was much, much older. I don't even know that they did baptisms there. We always went down to the river at [Cusie] Sullivan's Fish Camp at the end of Harrington. That's where the baptisms took place when I came along.

When I was growing up, you didn't have to look for fun like children now think of as fun. Everything was fun. You even made fun out of your homework. We played all over this area because there were no fence laws. We could go anywhere we wanted to without trespassing on anybody's property, and the people who were around didn't care. Everybody got along.

People used hand pumps to get water back then. I don't remember what year electricity came to the settlement. We all went to school at the little two-room schoolhouse in Harrington. When I started, it might have been one room, and then they changed it to two rooms. We're trying to make it a historical landmark. We really need it to remember Harrington.

When you finished the Harrington School, you had to walk down Frederica to the stables [at the intersection with the Sea Island Causeway, about two and a half miles away] just to pay your way on a city bus to get to school in Brunswick. My mother couldn't see that at all, having girls walk that distance twice a day to go to school. She sacrificed so that we could get away and go to boarding school at the Gillespie-Seldon Institute in Cordele, Georgia. I was thirteen when I left. I went away to boarding school in 1944, then to college and work.

I remember the Taylors and the Stevenses. Virginia Stevens is the one who cared for R. S.'s monument at the park [Fort Frederica] while they lived there, before it was a national park. They got kicked off of that land, just like people are trying to kick us off our land now. Everything has changed so drastically. It's happening everywhere, not just St. Simons. They don't want to see a green spot. When the last tree goes, we're all gone.

R. S.'s father [Tom] worked for the Stevens family. When R. S. started his newspaper and could afford to have that monument done, Mrs. Virginia Stevens took care of the monument because he sent her children to school. Why would he do that? He was honoring his father.[2]

R. S. also sent his family's nieces and nephews to college, up to a certain point. He is a relative, but the time we came along, we didn't get any of the money. There was a book about Robert Abbott, *The Lonely Warrior*. There was a documentary made about him called *The Paper Trail*,[3] about R. S. Abbott by Robert Abbott Sengstacke, a relative.

My house is right next to where Oglethorpe's house used to be, now Oglethorpe Memorial Gardens. I never found any artifacts from those days, but I can remember years ago there was what they called a "cow dip" behind the Oglethorpe Monument, where they dipped cows to get ticks off of them. But it's a part of the memorial gardens.

This is the third house that I've lived in on this plot of land, and I'm not selling. It's disgusting what you have to do—I can't eat for paying taxes—and every time you turn around someone is calling you about selling the property. And where do you go when you sell your home? People who sell don't think like that. All they can think of is the almighty dollar. And then where do you live? This is home, and I don't take that lightly. So many people in Harrington have given up their properties because they say they can no longer pay the taxes. But I tell them, "Get your priorities in order. If you'll stop buying new cars and smoking expensive cigarettes and trying to keep up with your neighbors, you can pay your taxes."

It's hard. I mean it is tough. People are buying property so they can make money from it. They're not attached to the land. It means nothing to them, and they don't care how that displaces people. They're doing the same thing in Brunswick. They call it "Blueprint Brunswick." They're going after the old houses, and they are dilapidated houses, but this is all poor people can afford. So they demolish those and build new units—stacking people one on top of the next—and they can't afford the rent. That's a legal way of pushing them even further down.

My parents sacrificed like crazy to keep us here. They had to sacrifice everything. With eleven children, what can you have, making less than minimum wages? And I'm doing the same thing now. And I pray to God every day that I can hold on, because it means a lot to me.

NOTES

1. Roi Ottley, *The Lonely Warrior: The Life and Times of Robert S. Abbott* (Chicago: Henry Regnery Company, 1955), 20–22. The author writes, "Captain Stevens . . . impetuously joined the Confederate Army. Like all affluent Southerners, he took along his body servant, Robert's uncle Randolph. . . . Randolph survived, but Captain Stevens was captured early and died of pneumonia in a Union prison camp somewhere in Virginia. . . . Randolph, now left to his own devices, enlisted in the

Confederate Army and served for the duration as a private in Company F, First Regiment of the Georgia Reserves. . . . When Randolph mustered out, he was entitled to $50 back pay which he never received, but he afterwards qualified to receive a Federal government pension as a Confederate veteran. Randolph . . . was content to marry, settle in Frederica, and raise a family. He had three sons—Joseph, Thomas, and Bristol. His grandson Randolph, a bachelor, today [1955] operates the Blue Island Tavern on the site of his inheritance; and his grandson Malcolm Lee Abbott . . . today lives with his wife and eleven children in a wooden frame house, where James Edward Oglethorpe, founder and first governor of Georgia, established his home in 1786."

2. Ibid., 17–18. Ottley notes that "Robert Sengstacke Abbott . . . was one of the first Negroes in the United States to become a millionaire. . . . Near Christ Church, a tall, gleaming shaft of white Quincy granite stands at the entrance to Fort Frederica. . . . The column, neatly enclosed by a grilled iron fence painted black, was erected at a cost of $1,600 by Robert S. Abbott as a monument to a slave he never knew: his father, Thomas Abbott. The site was chosen by the descendants of Tom's master, who buried him in 1869 with Christian ceremony, because he had been a faithful slave belonging to Captain Charles Stevens."

3. http://www.langstonblackfilmfest.org/JerryLarge.htm, accessed November 12, 2006. *Paper Trail: 100 Years of the* Chicago Defender was screened at the Langston Hughes African-American Film Festival.

Dr. Charles E. Pearson, 1946

Sarah "Sally" Elizabeth Taylor Jones
and Dr. Charles E. Pearson

Sally Jones, a lifelong resident of St. Simons, is the great-granddaughter of Captain Charles Stevens, a coasting captain who owned what is now Fort Frederica National Monument. Sally grew up at the town of Frederica, established in 1735 by Georgia's founder, General James Oglethorpe. Frederica, situated on an abandoned Indian field, was named in honor of Frederick, prince of Wales and father of King George III. Margaret Davis Cate describes Frederica as "the most expensive fortification built by the British in North America and . . . the military headquarters of this Southern Frontier for Britain's Colonies in the New World against the Spaniards in Florida."[1] In Georgia's Land of the Golden Isles, *Burnette Vanstory portrays Frederica as "a bustling military post . . . its streets peopled by British Regulars in their red coats and three-cornered hats; by*

Highlanders in plaids and bonnets; by Indians in moccasins and breech-clouts; by trader, merchant artisan; by townspeople with their sprinkling of courageous pioneer women, bravely flaunting the ruffles and 'ribbands' that caused their pious young pastor [Charles Wesley] such grave misgivings. . . . In the midst of it all was the aristocratic James Edward Oglethorpe, experienced military man and member of the House of Parliament."[2]

The Stevenses and the descendants of William Curtis Taylor built their homes there. Mrs. Jones's family lived at Frederica until the 1940s, when the land was handed over to the federal government and made into a national park.

Dr. Charles Pearson, Sally's nephew, is the grandson of Reginald Taylor, also of Frederica. Dr. Pearson has written several articles about the Stevens and Taylor families, including one in the Georgia Historical Quarterly *on Charles Stevens.[3] He talks about the coasting captains of Frederica, one of whom was James Frewin, who was born in London in 1781, served in the British navy for eighteen years, and eventually settled at Frederica, where he kept a tavern. Pearson credits Frewin and the Stevens and Taylor families for preserving much of the fort during almost 150 years of their occupation of Frederica. Dr. Pearson resides in Appomattox, Virginia.*

Sally: I was born May 4, 1939, at the hospital on the south end of Brunswick. My parents were Reginald Arnold Taylor, Sr., and Banford Bush. My father called me Sally. My mother's parents owned the Bush Docks on the south-end riverfront of Brunswick, where the Liberty ships were later built. Her family was from South Carolina. I think they loaded timber there. I grew up at Frederica on St. Simons. When my ancestors came from England, they were given that piece of property. They built a house on top of the original tabby fort. Later, they moved the family house to the bank of the Frederica River.

Charles: I was born when the Taylors and Stevenses were still living at Frederica. All of the Taylor men were born and raised at Frederica and lived their entire lives on St. Simons. Frederica used to be a steamboat landing until the 1920s [see the Eleanor Stiles Cate narrative]. The Taylors [Archibald, Douglas, Arthur, Charles, and Reginald] were true island men, making their living from their island lands and from the coastal waters. The great changes that occurred on St. Simons beginning around World War II essentially ended their way of life.

Sally: The boys at the Dodge Home [an orphans' home at Frederica] came to our house a lot, and we rode the bus with them to school. School was the St. Simons Elementary on the island. The principal was Mrs. Conley. When I came back to St. Simons after teaching in Atlanta, I taught at St. Simons Elementary.

For entertainment, we read a lot when I was young. Mother probably bought me and my sister, Isabelle, every Nancy Drew book there was. We played cards, walked in the woods, went on the river. We swam and rode horses. Mother was always feeding the family. Our nearest neighbor was a mile away—my father's brother, Douglas—and we very seldom went down to the pier section.

We saw plenty of alligators in the rivers. They ranged in size. We were out on the Hampton River this weekend and saw one that was immense. He had a tremendous head. He was probably ten or twelve feet.

We found all kinds of artifacts on the Frederica grounds—cannonballs, musket balls. There was an old well that they used as a dumping pit.[4] The Frederica residents just dumped whatever they had into it. A lot of the china pieces Mother found are now in the museum there at Fort Frederica.

Charles: My aunt Berta married my uncle Douglas Taylor. Aunt Berta was also Jim Gould's aunt [see the James Dunn Gould III and Mary Frances Young Gould narrative]. Prior to World War II, there weren't a lot of people to marry on St. Simons. I have lots of cousins there because a set of brothers married a set of sisters, a set of cousins married a set of cousins. Those were the days before they had a bridge. They had to go back and forth to the mainland by boat, and I guess it was easier to marry someone from the island. There were not a lot of permanent residents on the island in those days. In the 1850 census, there were probably not ten or twelve households listed on St. Simons.

Sally: When mother was a child, there were eight white families on the island. That was it. The rest were blacks.[5]

When I was growing up, we considered all the black families at Harrington like family because they had been there as long as we had. I remember Cusie and Ben Sullivan. I know Buck Buchanan, too. I love Buck. He's been here forever. He was a fantastic brick mason, the best I've seen in this area. He's selling figs now, if you know anyone on the island who wants to buy figs!

Charles: The Abbott family [see the Viola Vonceal Abbott narrative], a black family on the island, were slaves of Charles Stevens. Throughout the time when I was young, the Abbott family had a very close relationship with my grandmother and grandfather. They visited them a lot and fished for them. I've always been interested in their family history related to Charles Stevens owning members of their family. There's an Abbott Monument at Frederica. Robert Abbott was the son of one of the Stevens' slaves. He eventually

Sarah "Sally" Elizabeth Taylor Jones, 2006

Dr. Charles E. Pearson, 2007

grew up and moved to Chicago and started a newspaper called *The Defender* and became one of the wealthiest blacks in America. The Taylors and Stevenses let him put up a monument to his father [Tom] on their land at Frederica. There has been a biography written about Robert.[6]

Sally: For water, we used a well. I don't remember when electricity was put in there. My family lived at Frederica until the government condemned the property and took it from us. They wanted to make it into a national park. After that, we moved to Lawrence on the north end of the island when I was maybe six or seven.

Charles: By the 1960s, taxes and changing lifestyles on the island put an end to that traditional way of life. My grandfather bought the property that is now the Longview Shopping Center, but he never moved there because a whole series of disasters befell the family. First of all, they were run out of Frederica. When I talk to the people who run the Fort Frederica park now, they will not recognize that a viable community once lived there. They talk about it being a wilderness when the government took it over. There were ten or twelve houses there, one of which was the oldest house standing on St. Simons, and the park service went in and tore it down to establish the federal park. I'm not against the park, but you would never know that the oldest community on St. Simons was still active when it was made a national park.

A couple of the houses were moved. My uncle Doug moved his to Oatland. Charles Douglas Taylor moved one. They gave them six months to move the houses or have them torn down. You also read that the families donated the property to the government park service. They didn't donate it. They were threatened with confiscation and a lower price if they did not sign on the dotted line.

Sally: We lived at what is now Taylor's Fishing Camp, which was owned by my father and his brothers. There was nothing around us there. It was wonderful. We leased Butler's Point and Cannon's Point and raised hogs and cows there. They filmed the movie *Conrack*, which was based on *The Water Is Wide* by Pat Conroy, at Taylor's Fishing Camp. The little schoolhouse they built for the movie is still there. We had a very large two-story house that was built with heart-of-pine and pegs. Sea Island [the Sea Island Company] bought the property from Mother, and she moved. Sometime after that, lightning hit the house and of course torched it.

My father owned what is now Longview Shopping Center and Redfern Village. He bought that area to raise vegetables, but he let planes land there on his field [later named Redfern Field]. Papa divided that land up and gave it to his brothers and sisters.

My father's mother, Isabelle Stevens Taylor, gave a lot of the property to Christ Church. They called her "Belle." Howard Coffin used to come up to Frederica and talk to Grandmother about the history of the island. I've been going to Christ Church all my life.

I don't remember black congregations baptizing in the river at Frederica, but from what the family has passed down, they used to do that. They'd come up from the African Baptist church. Near Harrington, there used to be Obligation Pond. It's where you were obligated to stop and let your horses or oxen drink water when you were coming up to church. They'd let the ox go in there and drink. Then they'd buggy on up to Christ Church. They used to baptize in there, too, but it's been covered over with houses. It's no longer there.

Charles: I spent most summers from the 1940s to the 1960s on St. Simons. Some years, we lived there. When I would go, we'd stay with my grandparents at Lawrence, the old plantation, where Taylor's Fish Camp is. They bought Lawrence Plantation back from

Mrs. Dodge just after World War I. They opened a business called Taylor Brothers and raised cattle, farmed, took fishing parties out, and owned a few cottages on the south end. They pretty much ran their farming activities the way their grandfather and their uncle James Frewin had done—raised cattle and hogs in the wild.

Sally: My great-grandfather Charles Stevens was Danish, and his wife was British. Charles traded by ship up and down the coast during the War Between the States, or the War of Northern Aggression. He was captured and imprisoned at Pea Patch Island in the Delaware River, where he died. During the war, the family went over to Brunswick, where Belle Point is today. Captain James Frewin used to light a fire on top of the fort at night to let them know he was alive and still okay. The island was occupied by Yankee forces at that time. Of course, they stole everything the family had at Frederica and desecrated Christ Church.

Charles: Charles Stevens' uncle James Frewin worked as a coasting captain in the 1820s. From the late 1830s until the Civil War, Charles Stevens was engaged in local trade along the Georgia coast between St. Augustine and Port Royal, South Carolina. That was the area of activity of these traders after 1810. Prior to that, Charleston dominated the trade, but in the 18-teens, particularly after the War of 1812, Savannah began to capture more and more of the local planters' trade.

The coasting captains carried plantation goods into Savannah and Charleston and carried goods out. The Civil War destroyed the sailing trade. Steamboats kept going after that, but the sailing trade was essentially destroyed. At one time, there were several hundred sailing ships and five hundred captains involved in the trade. Some of the captains only sailed once or twice. A large percentage were New England men who came down and worked. But the vast majority of captains were foreigners like Frewin and Stevens. Southerners as a whole were not interested in maritime activity. Very few native-born Southerners served as captains.

James Frewin bought the fort in the 1820s, I believe from James Lawrence, another coasting captain. A whole series of coasting captains lived at the town of Frederica. My great-grandmother gave the Colonial Dames of Georgia the fort because she owned it. One of the deeds that I gave to the historical society is for the purchase of the old fort by the Frewins. By the time Frewin died, he left all of his land, about five hundred acres from Frederica almost to Harrington, to his nephew Charles Stevens.

James Frewin was an interesting character. Frewin has been spelled a number of ways—*Frewin, Fruin, Fruen,* or *Frowen.* He was a peg leg—he only had one leg—and his wife lost her leg in the hurricane of 1824. She got thrown off of a horse, and they had to amputate her leg, so it must have been an interesting sight to see this elderly couple, each with only two good legs between them.

The slaves left with the Stevenses, who rented them out to various families on the mainland. One of Stevenses' two-masted schooners, the *Northern Belle*—he renamed it the *Southern Belle*—was sunk in Frederica River during the Civil War. It was captured by the Union, and he was captured not long after that. He ended up dying as a prisoner of war at Fort Delaware. He's buried in New Jersey right opposite of Fort Delaware at a place called Finn's Point. There's a national cemetery there. James Frewin refused to leave the island during the occupation by Union soldiers during the Civil War. He didn't have a great sympathy for the Southern cause. Frewin was in his eighties at the time.

Not long ago, I had done some research online and got an e-mail from a woman who had purchased a letter from a Union naval officer who was stationed on St. Simons during the Civil War. He talked about Frewin's death. He sent a contingent of U.S. naval men to bury him at Frederica, where his tomb is now. Frewin's grandnephew Johnnie Stevens came down to the navy station, where the pier is now. He told the officer that Frewin had died and asked for help. The officer sent sailors to bury this Southerner at Christ Church, who had actually served in the British navy for about fifteen years, from the 1790s to the War of 1812.

The local captains knew the waters well enough that they typically did not use pilots. Most of them learned as mates or as young boys growing up on these boats. Stevens was the most active of the captains from the Brunswick–Glynn County area for many years. Many of the captains became pilots during the Civil War, working for both the Union and the Confederacy. Most Savannah residents don't want to know that their ancestors worked for the Union navy, but several did. They're hard-core Southerners now, but you look back in the record and their ancestors were being paid by the Union navy as active pilots.

Two local pilot families were the Brockintons and, nowadays, the Fendigs [see the Edwin Rubel Fendig, Jr., narrative]. The Brockintons were prominent coasting captains as far back as the 1840s and 1850s. Most of them were from Camden County, but they moved up to Glynn County by the 1850s. Captain Brockinton, who I knew as a kid, was nicknamed "Froggy." My grandfather, Sally's father, knew Captain Brockinton well. Captain Brockinton and his brothers were the last generation of real islanders. They lived on the water, and they had cattle. They ran cattle over probably half of St. Simons and Long Island, which is now Sea Island. Captain Brockinton and his first cousin Foreman Stevens were so familiar with the waterways that during World War I they were taken into the navy as ensigns and given immediate commissions to work on patrol boats out of Savannah. My grandfather Reginald Taylor eventually became the executive officer on a small boat out of Savannah.

Sally: We have more and more people coming down to the island now. They're spending ungodly amounts of money on houses and property. They have built subdivisions all through Harrington and are forcing our black friends out of there. Property taxes go up and up and up, and Frederica Road is a nightmare. The blacks are being run off the island, and it's not right.

Charles: Some of the black families on the island are selling their property because it looks like a lot of money, but it's slowly destroying the largest black community on any of the sea islands. They're all having to move to Brunswick. They can't afford to get another house on St. Simons. That's one of the reasons I don't like to come back to visit the island.

Sally: Anyone who owns a big piece of land is a threat. Frederica was a threat because you could build a complex there. It's the highest bluff on St. Simons. Sea Island [Company] is the master now.

NOTES

1. Orrin Sage Wightman and Margaret Davis Cate, *Early Days of Coastal Georgia* (St. Simons Island, Ga.: Fort Frederica Association, 1955), 11.

2. Burnette Vanstory, *Georgia's Land of the Golden Isles* (Athens, Ga.: Brown Thrasher Books, University of Georgia Press, 1956), 132.

3. Charles E. Pearson, "Captain Charles Stevens and the Antebellum Georgia Coasting Trade," *Georgia Historical Quarterly* 75 (1991), 485–506.

4. Vanstory, *Georgia's Land of the Golden Isles*, 141. Vanstory tells of the artifacts unearthed on the Frederica grounds: "In November 1951 work was begun on excavation of foundations of the old town. . . . Six filled-in wells were discovered, one packed to the brim with refuse that contained articles of inestimable value to archaeologists and historians. Among the whole and

fragmentary articles found in the excavations were pieces of hand-etched glassware, goblet stems with teardrop intact, and numerous fragments of porcelain and Delft. There were a few eighteenth-century English pennies and German coins, and an engraved nameplate that belonged to Captain Horton, discarded, no doubt, when he was promoted to the rank of major upon being placed in command of the troops at Frederica when General Oglethorpe returned to England in 1743."

5. Caroline Couper Lovell. *The Golden Isles of Georgia* (Little, Brown and Company, 1933), 269. Lovell accounts for some of the island's families: "After the [Civil] war but few of the old families returned to live on St. Simons. Retreat had been presented to the Negroes by the Federal soldiers, but was finally restored to the Kings, when it became the home of Colonel Mallory King and his family. . . . The Goulds were still at Black Banks, and Annie Cater, having married Mr. John Postell, was in her old home, Kelvyn Grove. The Stevenses and Abbotts were on the west side of the island, but everyone else had moved away, most of them going to Brunswick, which had now superseded Darien as a place of business."

6. Roi Ottley, *The Lonely Warrior: The Life and Times of Robert S. Abbott* (Chicago: Henry Regnery Company, 1955).

Allen Augustine Burns, Jr., 1940s

Allen Augustine Burns, Jr.

Allen Burns is a direct descendant of the Postell family, whose Kelvin Grove Plantation once encompassed the southeastern portion of St. Simons. He has the double distinctions of being twice evicted from island land by eminent domain and of residing on two tracts of historic ground—Frederica and German Village. German Village was settled in 1736 by German Lutherans, known as Salzburgers, who sold produce and fish to the Frederica settlers. The Salzburgers left the island after Oglethorpe's Regiment disbanded in 1749. German Village used to be called "the village" until the current village on the south end of the island came into existence.

Burns recounts rowing to nearby islands to gather turtle eggs, coon hunting, hurricanes, and life on St. Simons before refrigeration. He also recalls the sinking of two freighters, the Esso Baton Rouge *and the* Oklahoma, *by a German U-boat during World War II.*

I was born on January 26, 1929, in the old hospital on the south end of Brunswick on Norwich Street. My father, Allen, was an orphan and came from Atlanta to St. Simons as a child. He grew up at the Dodge Home for orphans at Frederica. Anson Dodge started the home, and his wife [Anna Gould Dodge] continued it. She was running it when my father was there. The Dodge family was from New England, and they were in the lumber business. The Dodge Home was in what is part of the Fort Frederica grounds now, inside of the moat.

My mother, Frances Postell Burns, was the oldest child of Clifford and Zoe Postell. The Postell family has been on St. Simons for generations. My great-grandfather James P. Postell came from Savannah. He married a local girl, Ann Armstrong Cater, who owned Kelvin Grove and a good number of slaves. He managed the estate and made a plantation of it before the Civil War. Ann Armstrong's mother was married to Benjamin Cater, whose father, Thomas, was killed by an overseer. The overseer and Thomas Cater's wife ran off and went north. Benjamin, the son, was taken by the slaves over to the King [Retreat] plantation, and they raised him.

Kelvin Grove, the Postell land, extended all the way from Oglethorpe Park south to the lighthouse on the east side of Frederica Road, and it included all of East Beach. Kelvin Grove is now a neighborhood where Bloody Marsh is, and the old Military Road runs through it.

My mother was a good friend of Eugenia Price and Joyce Blackburn. She gave them stories for some of the books they wrote. She was at the dedication of the F. J. Torras Causeway in 1924, which links St. Simons to Brunswick. There is an old photograph of her at the ceremony.

My grandmother's family came from Charleston. They were the

Allen Augustine Burns, Jr.

Simmons, who lived in Brunswick. Both of my great-grandfathers were in the Civil War. I've got the old army discharge papers from the Simmons side. I have a photograph of my Postell great-grandfather and his troop. He was a captain in the Confederate army. It's a funny picture because at that time they didn't have any uniforms, and he's wearing a top hat.

My grandfather Clifford Postell told the story of riding out a hurricane and seeing a log floating by with a rattlesnake on one end and a rabbit on the other. One of the worst hurricanes that hit here was in 1898. He told the story of putting his mother up in a tree at Kelvin Grove. The water came up, but she survived. The bottom of the house was trashed from mud and water.

When I was a young child, we lived almost right behind the Christ Church rectory near the East Beach Causeway, on what is now one of the McKinnon Airport runways. My grandfather also had a house there, but it was a little bit further east than ours and fronted on Demere Road. Behind our house was nothing but woods.

When they built the airport, we had to sell out to them, and we moved out to Fort Frederica in about 1936. I was probably five or six years old. We lived at the fort from about 1935 or 1936 until 1940 or 1941.

There were about ten or fifteen boys in the Dodge Home, located at Frederica, and we all played together. Back when I was young, we had the run of the island. I don't know what the population was then, but I knew most everybody on St. Simons. We'd go hunting and fishing on the north end of the island and encountered quite a few rattlesnakes. Occasionally, you'd come across old graves.

There were three graves on the west side of Lawrence Road between the African Baptist church and German Village. Back in the 1970s, there was a cult around here that would go out there and burn candles and whatnot. The tombstones were broken. Now, there's no sign of them.

I saw a lot of old tabby ruins way back in the woods a couple of miles north of West Point on the marsh edge. I have also come across Indian burial sites on the north island up at Hampton Point on the riverbank. I've also seen them in the German Village area on the riverbank. There were shell mounds when I was a kid between German Village and Taylor's Fish Camp. The Indians would come to the island and eat oysters and leave the shells behind in these mounds. I found a few arrowheads and clay things.

We'd also play on the fort's old barracks and dive off the old tabby fort into the Frederica River and swim. Back then, the river came right up to it. They have since built up the riverbank in front of the fort to keep it from crumbling into the river. There was a tomb that was at the end of our property, which is still there. We would go in there and catch bats. I remember there was one cannon out there left over from Oglethorpe's days. We didn't know the original colonial Fort Frederica home foundations were right there under us. At that time, Frederica Road went all the way down to the river next to the fort. Frederica Road forked at our house, and part of it went up to the Pink Chapel.[1]

There were seven or eight framed houses at Frederica then, which were torn down after the fort became a national park. Our house was just about where the parking lot entrance to Fort Frederica is now. It was originally an old schoolhouse. Between the fort and the old tabby barracks, which is east of the fort, Arthur Taylor had a home. Mr. Taylor had four children. On the north side of the main road coming back away from the fort was his brother, Reginald Taylor, who ran Taylor's Fish Camp with Arthur. He also had four children. Across the street from him was Douglas Taylor, who was the caretaker for Little St. Simons. He was married to

Berta Gould, who was Jimmy Gould's aunt [see the James Dunn Gould III and Mary Frances Cannon Gould narrative]. The house next to Reg's was Archibald Taylor's, who ran the Sea Island Fish Camp, which was on the north end of Sea Island back in the 1930s. The next home on that side of the road was the Dodge Home. And the next home was our house. Across the street from us was Elliott Stevens. He had two daughters and a son. The Stevens boys ran a garage where Strother's Hardware is now. They were always playing tricks on people. They had a package they rigged up with some sort of an electrical charge. If someone came by, they'd hand it to him or her and say, "Please mail this for me." Of course, when the person grabbed the package, it would shock him.

In those days, you had either kerosene lamps or pump-up gas lamps, or kerosene stoves or wood stoves. We had septic tanks and hogs to take care of food scraps. Every house had an artesian well. There was enough pressure that you could get water in the house. To give you an idea of how much water pressure we had, when I was a boy, near the ruins of the old original Island Hotel where Massengale Park is now, there was a pipe that went thirty feet up in the air, and water would come out of the top of that pipe. It had that much pressure. The aquifer in this area used to be around six hundred feet. Before that, people had open wells. Old Mrs. Stevens had the last open well that I can remember. It was probably three feet in diameter and bricked all around and down at least twenty feet. They'd drop a bucket down there and get their water.

Back then, our phone was on a party line. So many rings was your number. If there were five people sharing the party line, you'd have one ring, two rings, three rings, four rings, and five rings. I can't remember which ring we were. Everything on the island was a lot slower pace. Everyone knew everyone else. We never locked houses or had to worry about leaving a boat on the riverbank.

First, we lived where McKinnon Airport is now. That land was condemned by the government to build the airport. That was a government job. Then we moved to Fort Frederica. That land was condemned by the government to make it a national park. We had to move twice due to eminent domain. It wasn't called that then. From Frederica, we moved to a house in Glynn Haven. We fished and swam in Ebo's Landing.

My family moved to German Village in the 1950s. It was named German Village after German Salzburgers, who came here as mercenaries for General Oglethorpe. They built a settlement here, of which nothing is left.

My father operated the Glynn Ice Company on St. Simons, in the village by the pier. There were no refrigerators back then. The ice was made in Brunswick and stored on the island. The icehouse had thick walls and a compressor that kept everything cold. There were at least two ice trucks that went out every morning. They had a route that served different sections of the island. The icehouse is now part of a gift shop in the village [at the south end of the village].

Dad also drove one of the two island school buses. He'd drive the bus to school in the morning, come back and work the icehouse, then go back to Brunswick in the afternoon. Dad kicked me off the bus one time. I got a little rowdy, and he didn't stand for that, so he put me off in the middle of the causeway. I had to walk home.

One time back in the '40s during a hurricane, they let school out. We had to come back across the causeway on a bus, and the wind was blowing pretty good, and the tide was up. The school superintendent, Mr. Wanamaker, followed the school bus in his car to make sure we got across. At some point, we had to stop, and he ran into the back of the bus. We did get across, though, and survived the hurricane.

I had a paper route at one time. I'd come home from school

and ride my bicycle to the corner of Frederica and Sea Island roads, where I'd pick up my papers. Then I rode over to Sea Island, where I had clients—the Joneses and Levys and others, all the way down to Thirty-sixth Street. I'd ride back and go north on Frederica Road. I had a few customers in Glynn Haven, and then there was nothing until you got up to Harrington, where my black customers lived—Whings, Sullivans [see the Carolyn Evangeline Whitfield and Bernice Wilma Myers narrative], Hunters, and Ramseys. Then I'd go to South Harrington and then cut across and come back on North Harrington. The whole route took about two or three hours to complete. I'd get home in the dark in the wintertime. I guess I had forty or fifty customers back then. When my father died, Bully Ramsey came up to visit me and told me that my father dying was the only white man he'd cried about.

Since there were several mean dogs on my route that chased and tried to bite my legs, I carried a water pistol filled with ammonia. One shot in the face and I was never bothered again. If fact, they ran the other way.

One of the ways I'd make money was I'd take a .22 rifle and hunt coons. I'd skin them and dry the hides and sell the hides and meat down to the people in Harrington. I think I sold them for fifty cents apiece.

Some of the black people on the island were very superstitious. If someone saw a black cat, he'd turn around three times and spit over his shoulder. Some people kept frizzle chickens in the yard to keep ghosts and haints away from them.

Black folks held baptisms in the ocean at the beach. Down next to Harrington, there was a pond they called Obligation Pond, right on the edge of Frederica Road. It was where you got rid of your sins and took on your obligations. The pond was on the west side of the road as you go north on Frederica, past Benny's Red Barn on the left. There is now a little subdivision on that spot. The first house on your right when you go in that subdivision is right over Obligation Pond. Some developer filled it in and built on it. My wife [Angie Burns] wrote a poem about it:

Sins, Past and Present

She was baptized in Obligation Pond,
Her white dress billowing about her small frame.
Sins accumulated in her short life
Swam free in the depths of Obligation,

Joining other sins having been released.
Brother Jones, waist-deep in the brown water,
Dipped her braided head below the surface.
Emerging, she rubbed her eyes—sputtering,

Ridding herself of every remnant left
Of youthful evil. Her Ma and Pa cried,
And all the folks in their Sunday-best clothes
Shouted "Hallelujah" from the pond banks.

Years passed. Obligation Pond shrank in size,
Condensing sins, gradually leaving them
Trapped in small pools of mosquitoey mud;
To be forgotten except by old ones.

Land developers with no respect for
Past or future are filling what is left
Of Obligation—packing down its sins,
Disregarding wetland preservation,

But, oh the woe! Of living just above
A place where sins are bound to bubble up,

To seep into the crevices of homes
And manifest themselves on children's children.

I met my wife, Angie, after she came to Brunswick from Pineview, Georgia. She was a teacher at Goodyear School. A friend of mine dated her one night, and I joined them at a club when I got off of work. We danced, and I asked her out on a date, and things progressed from there.

One of my memories during World War II was waking up in the middle of the night when the Germans torpedoed two ships offshore. You could hear it from our house at Fort Frederica. It was a heck of a blast. There were two blasts, as a matter of fact. I remember when they towed one of the ships into the St. Simons Sound. It was anchored out there for a long time. There was a hole in the ship big enough to drive a truck through, where that torpedo hit.

There was a gas station where Bruce Faircloth's shop [in the village] used to be, which Sam Cofer ran during World War II. I was in high school during the war and worked at that service station. I used to go down and talk to the guys riding beach patrol on horses. They'd tell me a few things they'd seen. The Coast Guard had horse patrols that rode Sea Island beach, St. Simons beach, and Jekyll beach day and night. We didn't have a fear of being invaded.

We'd go on the beach turtle egg hunting and find a life vest or things like that floating up on the shore. Back then, sea turtles were numerous. On Little St. Simons and Jekyll Island beaches, there was a sea turtle crawling every hundred yards. We would row across to Jekyll or Little St. Simons and walk the beach at night. Back then, it was legal to get turtle eggs. You boiled them with a lot of pepper. The eggs never do get hard. They look like a Ping-Pong ball, but they're soft. The yoke would get a little bit hard. You'd tear the skin and suck the egg out of there when they were boiled. They made wonderful cakes. My wife, Angie, didn't like them. It's against the law to collect sea turtle eggs now.

I've been going to Christ Church all of my life. When I was a young boy in the church choir, we all vied to crank the church organ. There was no electricity at that time, so we had to hand-crank it. You sat back of the organ and cranked it the whole time the organist was playing. That was the premier job. All the boys wanted to do that.

My friends and I would take girls to Christ Church at night to scare them in that graveyard. One particular time I remember, when it was Halloween, we overheard this guy at a party telling some girls he was going to take them to Christ Church and show them a bust, which looked ghostly in the dark inside the church. So three or four of us left early and got there before them. There are some old, flat gravestones right next to the church. We laid on the gravestones and pulled sheets over us. And when they came to look into the window of the church and see that little bust, we moaned and raised up on those tombstones. You would have thought a herd of buffalo were trying to get out of there, screaming and running into things. Two of the girls ran into each other and knocked themselves out. They had big bumps on their heads. That really scared me, and we didn't do it again after that.

My grandfather told me he used to walk from Kelvin Grove to visit the Taylors at Fort Frederica. Sometimes, he was late coming back. One night, he was walking home and passing the graveyard at Christ Church. All of the sudden, something raised him off of the ground. He said if he had come off on the other side, he would have gone back to the Taylors'. But he came off on the home side and ran back to his house. What happened is he had come across a cow lying down in the middle of the road.

Maxfield Parrish's wife, Lydia Parrish, lived down at Bloody Marsh. She recorded a lot of the old slave songs.[2] I remember as a kid going down there and listening to her record them. She had a little cabin built out in front of her house on the edge of Demere Road, and that's where she did all of her recording. They did dances, and I guess she wrote descriptions of that. I don't remember her taking any pictures. Maxfield only came to the island occasionally. Lydia was down here every year with her two sons. There was a book titled *Maxfield Parrish*, by Coy Ludwig.[3] My father gave him some information for that book and is mentioned in the preface.

NOTES

1. Orrin Sage Wightman and Margaret Davis Cate, *Early Days of Coastal Georgia* (St. Simons Island, Ga.: Fort Frederica Association, 1955), 49, 51. The authors discuss the origin of Pink Chapel: "Rather than attend and worship at Christ Church, Frederica, the Hazzards erected their own family chapel at West Point Plantation. A beautiful pink lichen, *Chiodecton sanguieneum*, which grows only in dense shade on old walls and trees, now colors the old tabby ruins of the Hazzard Chapel, giving it the name Pink Chapel."

2. Ibid., 145. The authors write, "Mrs. [Lydia] Parrish became interested in the singing of the Negroes and . . . recorded these spirituals and 'shouts' and saved them for posterity in the publication of her excellent book, *Slave Songs of the Georgia Sea Islands*. By insisting that the Negroes sing in the old-fashioned way Mrs. Parrish created in their minds a feeling of respect for the songs of their ancestors. She held 'sings' at the cabin she built for this purpose and made it possible for visitors to enjoy them."

3. Coy Ludwig, *Maxfield Parrish* (New York: Watson-Guptill Publications, 1973).

Sonja Olsen Kinard

Sonja Kinard is a local writer and historian who grew up on historic Gascoigne Bluff—the site of Georgia's first navy, the site of the invading Spanish fleet's landing in 1742, and the location of live oak trees harvested to build the USS Constitution, *also known as "Old Ironsides." The bluff is also the location of Hamilton Plantation, on which two slave cabins still stand, as well as the location of post–Civil War lumbermills.*

During World War II, the United States Navy used Gascoigne Bluff to load and unload men and cargo. Sonja and her older sister, Thora Olsen Kimsey, compiled a book of area residents' recollections, entitled Memories from The Marshes of Glynn: World War II.

Her family, like others on the island, came from Scandinavia. Sonja recounts her grandparents' move from Norway to America, river baptisms, her father's work for tobacco heir R. J. Reynolds, Jr., and Coca-Cola heir Charles Candler, and island life during World War II.

My grandfather Olsen came to St. Simons on a ship in 1898 and decided to stay and work at the Dodge Mills on Gascoigne Bluff. My grandmother came over in 1900. They were from Grimstad, Norway. They had seven children, five of whom lived to adulthood. Two of the girls were born in Norway. Sophie was five years old the day they landed in Brunswick Harbor, July 9, 1900, and Antoinette was three. My father, Olaf Helmer Olsen, Sr., was the first child born in America. Other siblings born in the United States were Haakon, Olga, James Foster, and Martin Luther. The latter two died as infants. Antoinette died of pneumonia when she was in her twenties. Only Olaf, Haakon, Sophie, and Olga lived to adult life and married and had children. My dad was born at the Dodge Mills on St. Simons Island, April 16, 1901.[1]

When the mills on St. Simons closed, I think about 1906, they moved to Brunswick and lived on Cook Street at the end of the causeway. He ran away to sea when he was thirteen years old and was a cabin boy on a sailing ship. By the age of sixteen, he was back in Brunswick working in a shipyard. He boarded with the blind Lutheran minister, Charles Weltner, and his wife, Augusta, because he and his father had had a disagreement about who kept my father's pay.

My mother, Lillie Mae Quick, was from Lexington County, South Carolina. Her father died of smallpox when she was two years old. Her mother, Julia, worked in the Olympia Textile Mills in Lexington and Richmond counties in South Carolina. When she was eleven years old, my grandmother couldn't earn a living to take care

Sonja Olsen Kinard, circa 1930

of her, so with the help of the Lutheran minister and his wife, she went to the Lutheran Children's Home in Salem, Virginia. This was the same Lutheran pastor my father was living with in Brunswick in 1917. My mother stayed and went to a couple of years of college at Elizabeth College in Roanoke, Virginia. When she left, she went to Columbia to be with her mother, but this didn't work out, so Pastor and Mrs. Weltner invited her to come to Brunswick. That is how she and my father met. Dad was sixteen, and Mother was nineteen years old.

I was born in the Brunswick Hospital, Friday, October 13, 1933, the fourth and last child of Olaf Helmer and Lillie Mae Quick Olsen. Virginia was the oldest sibling, then Olaf, Jr., who we call "Bubber," then Thora, and me. Thora is the one who got the idea to put together *Memories from The Marshes of Glynn: World War II*.[2]

I grew up on Gascoigne Bluff on St. Simons, down the road from where my father had been born. I was born when my father was dockmaster at the Sea Island Yacht Club, so except for a seven-month period when Daddy worked on Sapelo Island for Mr. R. J. Reynolds [Jr.], I lived on that bluff until I got married.

We'd walk to Demere Road to catch the school bus. On cold and rainy days, we snuggled inside the old clapboard tollhouse, which was located at the end of the causeway on the Frederica River on St. Simons. One of the tollkeepers was Mr. Chitty. Al Burns was our school bus driver. We had two school buses to bring the children off the island to Brunswick. Elementary and high-school children rode the same bus. People crossing the causeway from Brunswick to St. Simons paid a toll at the booth on the St. Simons side of Terry Creek. They would get a ticket there and stop at the tollhouse on the other side of Frederica River on St. Simons and give the ticket to the tollhouse keeper to prove they had paid the toll. He also was responsible for opening the drawbridge when a boat wanted passage.

The original St. Simons Causeway opened in June 1924. The bridges over the Back and Frederica rivers were drawbridges, where the middle section pivoted around to open the bridge for the boats to pass. Mrs. Allen [Frances Postell] Burns was one of the people at the dedication of the causeway designed and built by engineer Fernando Torras.

During World War II, so many people moved to the area that they opened an elementary school on St. Simons on East Beach at Camp Marion. I was in the fifth grade that year. Fraser Ledbetter was my teacher. I went there for about two weeks. Since we lived on the west side of the island, I was transferred to school in Brunswick at Sidney Lanier Elementary, where I had attended the preceding four years. That year, we had to go to school in shifts because of the influx of so many people, military and mostly shipyard workers. When the semester changed, students who were going in the morning went in the afternoon, and vice versa. I could go only in the morning, since I rode the school bus. Afternoon sessions didn't get out until 5 P.M. Sidney Lanier Elementary, Prep High, and the high school, Glynn Academy, were right there together. Now, all of that compound is the Glynn Academy High School. When I was in the sixth grade, they opened the St. Simons Elementary School, and I attended the sixth grade there.

I remember two oil tankers were sunk off the coast by German U-boats. The next day, the *Esparta*, a cargo ship, was sunk off of Cumberland Island. It was a United Fruit Company boat. It sunk and is still there. It's called "the wreck," but I don't think there were any casualties on that one. I never knew of the third ship sunk until my sister and I did research on our book.[3]

We had to make our own entertainment when I was growing up. I played with Woodie Estes, who was my age. She had cerebral palsy, and we managed to have a good time. My sister Thora used to play with some of the black children who lived in Jewtown.

The black people from Jewtown used to hold baptisms in front of our house on Gascoigne Bluff. Someone would go out and measure the water. Of course, it would have to be at high tide. They would march down the road from Jewtown dressed in white. The people would stand on the bank and sing. Those being baptized were taken into the river and baptized.

We didn't have air conditioning. In the summer, we'd go down to the old Casino by the pier to play, visit, and stay cool. On one side of the Casino was a bowling alley with a soda fountain and a jukebox. The bowling alley eventually became the library. Fraser Ledbetter was the librarian there for many years. On the other side of the Casino was the movie theater. In the middle was a sunken area that had been intended for a swimming pool, but they ran out of money, so I was told. That area had a good floor for dancing. After I came back to St. Simons, the county had roughed the floor and planted greenery in the corner. The jukebox was on the sidelines of the dance floor. It was a fun place for the teenagers and the house parties that came from Macon and Atlanta in the summer. People danced and danced until the Casino closed for the evening. During the war, the soldiers thoroughly enjoyed dancing with the young girls. The jitterbug was the popular dance then. The playground with swings and sliding boards was out front. That is where I went. Mother sat on the sidelines visiting with other mothers. Since we all went our separate ways when we got to the pier, when ten o'clock came, Mother would toot the car horn, and we'd all come running.

The movies would change three times a week. In the winter, I'd go see a movie every week. It cost me twelve cents as a child. Black folks would have to go to the balcony of the Ritz Theatre on Newcastle Street in Brunswick to see a movie. There was also the Bijou Theatre on the other end of Newcastle.

By the time I came along, the old Dodge Mills were gone. There was a dairy there instead. Hamilton Plantation was owned by Eugene

Sonja Olsen Kinard

Lewis from Michigan, who was probably a friend of Howard Coffin. They had a swimming pool and lots of little fountains and a dock. Across from our house were two old slave cabins, which are the meeting houses of the Cassina Garden Club. They had a fountain there. Once, my sister Thora fell into it wearing her wool coat!

When Daddy worked as the dockmaster at the Sea Island Yacht Club, located on the south side of the causeway, the Sea Island Company had a restaurant, tennis courts, and a beautiful sunken garden. On the north side of the causeway, in front of our house on Gascoigne Bluff, was the Sea Island Boat Club, where people stored their boats. Daddy owned a couple of boats and rented them. Daddy also owned a boatyard in Brunswick on Terry's Creek in the early 1940s. During World War II, the Georgia State Guard commandeered boats that were docked there.

When R. J. Reynolds [Jr.] bought Sapelo Island from Howard Coffin—probably because Mr. Coffin needed cash to develop Sea Island—Daddy went to work for Mr. Reynolds, and we all moved over to Sapelo. There was a little school over there where Thora started first grade. My great-aunt Thora Pedersen, who had come over from Norway with Grandma, went to Sapelo with us. She had stayed in America and married Edwin Wallace, who had worked at the sawmills.

My brother Bubber was eight years old when we went to Sapelo [see the Olaf Helmer "Bubber" Olsen, Jr., narrative]. He had a billy goat, and one time Mr. Reynolds fed his billy goat beer. It went around butting everything. Bubber got so mad that he stomped to Mr. Reynolds' house and told him to stop giving his goat beer. I am told that there was too much partying and drinking going on, so Daddy left and brought us back to St. Simons. He had a wife, four children, and no job.

In the meantime, Charles Howard Candler, whose father started the Coca-Cola Company, bought the Cumberland Island Hotel on the north end of Cumberland. So Daddy started working for him as captain of the yacht and overseer of the property they had over there. He stayed in a room in the hotel during the summer and winter when on the island. It was cold because the hotel didn't have heat. Up until that time, our family never went over to Cumberland because there was no place for us to stay. As the Bensons, Faders, Burbanks, Bunkleys, Tomlinsons, and other families left Cumberland, Mr. Candler bought more land on the north end. He promised Daddy some land, and in 1959 he gave it to him. My father and four black men from Sapelo Island cut down the trees, sawed the lumber, and built a house there. The first summer we used it was in 1961. Dad only got to use it six years. He died in 1967.

There are mounds on Cumberland that are Indian burial sites. Most of the Indians' oyster shell middens were used up during the 1800s to make tabby. However, there is one midden on the south end of the island near Dungeness. The Cumberland Indians, the Timucua, were mound builders. When anyone died, they piled dirt on top of them. They didn't dig a hole for them. On the northwest side of Cumberland, there is a high bluff on the river. I don't know if that is a natural bluff or an Indian mound, or if Oglethorpe built it up for a fort.

It is so discouraging to see the destruction of St. Simons. The cause is greed. People are moving in from all over the United States because they like the climate, the beauty of the island, and the atmosphere. But they are causing everything but the climate to change. The black culture is being pushed out because of taxes. The longtime residents are being forced to sell their homes and move to Brunswick. Condominiums and houses are being built everywhere. Large oaks are being moved or cut down. I guess they call that progress.

1. Abbie Fuller Graham, *Old Mill Days: St. Simons Mills, Georgia, 1874–1908* (Brunswick, Ga.: St. Simons Public Library, Glover Printing Company, 1976). "In the years following the Civil War the Coastal Islands were in a more or less critical condition," Graham writes. "It was at this time that Norman W. Dodge, son of William E. Dodge, the philanthropist of New York City, and Titus B. Meigs of N.Y. decided to start a lumber mill on St. Simons."

2. Thora Olsen Kimsey and Sonja Olsen Kinard, *Memories from The Marshes of Glynn: World War II* (Decatur, Ga.: Looking Glass Books, 1999).

3. Ibid., A-32. Kimsey and Kinard report that "the 3,365 gross ton SS *Esparta* was torpedoed without warning at 0115 EWT on April 9, 1942 twelve miles S.E. of the buoy at St. Simons' Sound (30.46 N-81.11 W. midnight position). . . . The *Esparta* was en route from Puerto Cortez, Honduras, to New York with a cargo of bananas, coffee and miscellaneous goods."

Gloster Lewis "Buck" Buchanan

A farmer turned bricklayer who moved from Hazlehurst to St. Simons in 1934 "for something better," Buck Buchanan talks in this narrative about former slaves he knew who lived in the community of Jewtown, one of three settlements on St. Simons founded by freedmen. Here, he recalls a time when Georgia politics was dominated by Eugene Talmadge, famous for proclamations such as "The poor dirt farmer ain't got but three friends on this earth: God Almighty, Sears Roebuck, and Gene Talmadge."

As a skilled brick mason, Buchanan helped build many homes still standing on the island and restored brickwork on the kitchen ovens at John Couper's plantation at Cannon's Point. He's one of the last—if not the last—living person who knew Howard Coffin, the founder of the Sea Island Company with his cousin, Alfred Jones. Buchanan talks about race relations, life on the island during the Depression, and his father's curative powers.

❁ ❁ ❁

I was born on the 6th of June in 1916 in Jeff Davis County—Hazlehurst, Georgia—out in the country and raised in Wheeler County. It's a long story how we came about. My father was named Jeff Davis Buchanan. My mama was a McRae. There's a long history to my family. In fact, I'm writing a book about my family and my life. I got a history that nobody's got. I've got a history on my mama's side from slavery, and I got a history from my father's side clean back from slavery and who their master was and all through the war and how they came up and how we got the name of Buchanan. We got the name Buchanan in 1865 at freedom. My folks' slave master was named Silas Haddox. They were from up there around Hazlehurst. I got some people in my family that's carrying a history over two hundred years on height—six-foot-four and six-foot-six—that still runs in that family.

My grandmother was a full-blooded Cherokee Indian. Her name was Maria Haddox. All slaves went under the name of their slave master. My grandmother lived to 123. She drank hot water. It tastes bad. I tried some and spit it back out. That's all she'd drink. Some people didn't believe she was that old, but all the history we ever had taught that she was that old. She never was sick. She was a little woman. Had straight hair rolled up on top of her head. She died in 1930.

My father died in 1933. Then my uncle Lewis McRae raised me in Scotland, Georgia, south of McRae. I'm named after him. My cousin from Atlanta named me after a famous doctor, Dr. Gloster. I didn't like that name until I went into the service, when I met a Dr. Gloster. Then I started liking that name.

They've named me "Buck" since I came down here to St. Simons in 1934. I worked on my uncle's farm during the Depression, planting

Gloster Lewis "Buck" Buchanan

cotton, corn, watermelon—different things like that. The last year I farmed was 1934. Gene Talmadge, Herman's father, used to come talk to the people around McRae. He'd be talking about crops, and someone would say, "Hey, Gene! What about the niggas?" And Gene would start talking about roads, and someone would yell, "Hey, Gene! What about the niggas?"[1]

When I first came here, most black people couldn't vote in the state of Georgia—nowhere. When I came here, I registered and started voting. Nobody paid no attention. All the people get in a line—all the whites get in a line and the blacks get in that same line and vote. We'd vote down to the pier at the Casino. What it was, get in line, and they'd talk with you and everything. Mr. Bacchus Magwood would take his walking stick and walk down there [approximately two miles] and vote. That was back in 1936. I voted for [Franklin] Roosevelt. Anybody you wanted to vote for, you'd get in that line and vote. I don't know if I voted for Talmadge or not.[2] He's a man I knowed real well. He's from McRae.

I came to St. Simons looking for something better. I had some nieces and nephews living down here. There used to be a train that run from Atlanta to Brunswick. Anywhere up and down that line you could catch the train. You could leave here tonight and come back the next morning on the train. It took me about four or five hours by train to get here. It would stop at small places. I loved train travel. Go to Atlanta, see my people, and come back by train. It was good traveling. Brunswick had a depot on the waterfront on Bay Street. The train would back into there.

There are two things they shouldn't have never torn down, and that was the old train station and the old Oglethorpe Hotel. They should have never torn them down.

The people here couldn't pronounce Buchanan, so they called me "Buck." I met my wife, Celia, down here. She was a Mitchell. She was from right here. John Mitchell was her father. He was originally from Everett City, way back before Hilton and Dodge [lumbermills]. We were married in 1940. My daughter is Carol B. Walker.

I worked for the Sea Island Company back in 1935 at the hotel. They were paying something like twenty cents an hour. You worked nine hours, five days and a half, for about $9.45. I tended lawns, did landscaping. I'm the onliest man living that knowed Mr. Howard Coffin. He was kind of a big, tall man. Had a green Hudson automobile. He was a dealer for the Hudson Automobile Company. He always wore a green jacket. And that's where the Sea Island Company gets green from. I think he was from Akron, Ohio. He died in 1937. I went to his funeral at Christ Church.

The whole Jones family treats me like one of the family. I knowed all the Jones and all of the chil'ren when they was real small. Bill Jones was born about 1930. He was about five years [old] when I started working there. I worked for Sea Island for about five or six years and got laid off because it was so rough for them 'til they weren't hardly able to pay off. Sometimes, they paid off in scrips, a little piece of paper that's got some reading on it—twenty-five cents—because they didn't have any money. You took the scrip to a store and traded it in just like a check. There was a store in Glynn Haven called Mighty Fine. The man's name was Dan Cowart. He sold groceries and stuff. You could carry your scrip down there and trade it just like you would a check. Wasn't no banks over here.

It was so rough. A lot of people don't know that. I've got some of the scrips now. Young people don't know nothing about that. It was just rough. There wasn't no money! And when I tell people the Sea Island Company had such a rough time, they back up, take four or five steps backward. "You mean to tell me the Sea Island was having a rough time?" Well, I tell you, people don't know nothing about the Depression. When there wasn't no money. That's what it is.[3]

There weren't no jobs. Weren't no money. Everybody was poor. The people that owned land here, the taxes weren't very much, but there wasn't no work. You worked for Sea Island, maybe Arthur True, or Captain Brockinton.

People on St. Simons didn't have no money. Didn't have no jobs either, no more than what you worked for the Sea Island Company or for people that come down from Atlanta that had money. They worked people on their yard or do things like that. It was rough.

Back in slavery, back to Cannon's Point [John Couper's plantation], there's some chimneys standing up there that the slaves built—been standing there for two hundred years. In slavery time, they used to build the kitchen off from the house, so if the kitchen catches fire the house doesn't burn down. I went up there and repaired the old oven when I was working for the Sea Island Company, who owned the land. I worked for Sea Island the first job I had. Then I laid bricks for nearly thirty-five years. And the last job I had was with Sea Island. I worked for them in transportation about twelve years as a driver, taking people to Jacksonville or Savannah or wherever. Drove limousines, vans, buses. Go to the airport and pick up people and bring them back to the hotel. That was from 1982 'til about '91. That was the best job I ever had in my life. I made more money. The tips were good. They paid me a good salary. Six-fifty an hour and tips. Made more money than when I laid bricks.

Age will stop you. I tend my garden. I've a fig orchard—forty trees. I sell figs. Been selling figs for thirty years. Put a sign out there, and people stop and get them.

I worked in the shipyard here for a while during World War II. It was the Liberty ship yard, J. A. Jones Construction. I worked in the medical department driving an ambulance, picking up people from off of the ways [inclined structures on which ships are built], people who were injured building the ships. You'd have to carry them to the real hospital. The hospital was down on the south end of Brunswick then. The shipyard had a clinic and doctors—Dr. Hancock and Dr. Cole—and nurses. If we had a bad injury, we carried them to the city hospital.

You might get a broken leg or a broken arm or a flash burn from welding. If you get a leg broke, the doctor would set it, and I'd put on a cast. We had a few get killed out there. Some of them would fall off into the way or off a crane.

I'm a World War II veteran. I went in 1943 in the Army Air Corps and came out in 1947. I used to work for Mr. A. C. Oliver way back. I came out of the service and laid bricks. I've done work for Mr. Brockinton. I knowed him real good. A good friend of mine. A good man. I worked for him, and Mr. Arthur True, too. I got my start laying bricks for Mr. A. C. Oliver [see the Sara Evelyn Blackwell Oliver narrative].

Robert Wilson, my wife's brother, was a professional golfer. He used to teach people on the Sea Island Golf Course. He'd caddy out there. He was so good until it wasn't nothing. Back in them days, wasn't nothing for us—for blacks. The Sea Island Company would let him play after five o'clock.

I've lived in Jewtown the whole time I've been on St. Simons. Long years ago, there was a family here by the name of Levine [or Levison]. They had a store in Jewtown. That was during the lumbermill days on St. Simons, maybe before. The store was located just west of the [St. Ignatius] Episcopal church on the same side of Demere Road. It was just a big one-story building. There were two Jews in there. They stayed in there and sold groceries, horse collars, anything you want. It was a dilapidated building when I got here. There was a little piano in there. A fellow used to come in and play, and we'd have dances and things like that. Then it finally just went down.

I belonged to the St. Paul Baptist Church. We used to baptize people in MacKay River on the left-hand [south] side. We had a kind of a beach there we could just walk out on. We walked and drove to get there. The bridges were wooden at that time. The Brunswick Causeway didn't get concrete bridges until 1948.

All the black people on St. Simons years ago were slaves. There were big cotton plantations here—Retreat, Butler's Point, Gould's, and Postell's. That's where that comes from. There's a Gould Cemetery and a Village Cemetery. Musgrove Plantation's got a black cemetery there. Musgrove belonged to the Reynolds.

Some of the Jewtown people were Gould slaves. Most of them were from Retreat. They've been on the island a long time. Back from the slaves. Way back. When I came here, the black people owned all of Jewtown, clean up there across the road. I know all the people who owned this land. All the land on the south end, and Frederica, too. I can tell you the names of them, what they owned, and where it's at.

The Union Cemetery used be called the Strangers Cemetery. Long years ago, when former slaves where working the Hilton and Dodge Mills, some of them died, and they buried them in that cemetery—"Unknown." They didn't have no ties with anybody here on the island. The people that were born and raised here on the island didn't bury [there]. They didn't mix with the strangers. They mostly kept to themselves. The people here, they called the Gullah. That's the reason they called it the Strangers Cemetery, because most of the people buried there were not from here. But now, there are people raised right here on St. Simons buried there, like the Lifes and the Johnsons—Adrian Johnson and all them. Now, it's called Union Cemetery. I'm an executor of the cemetery. The Sea Island Company gave us more ground there. We named it Union Cemetery. I'll be buried there. They can't tax you out of there, but they'd like to. They've got houses all around it. Some people throw their yard trash over in our cemetery. We're going to see Mr. Bill Jones and tell him what's happening. He can make things happen because they shouldn't do that.

St. Ignatius Episcopal Church was built by the Hilton and Dodge Lumber Company for the black folks. I went to that church but didn't ever join.

All this land that you see around here [Demere Road from Frederica Road to Union Cemetery] belonged to blacks. This land [where the McDonald's restaurant now stands on the south side of Demere Road] belonged to people named Whitehead. Jasper Barnes owned the land next to it. He was related to Neptune Small [see the Neptune Small and Diane Cassandra Palmer Haywood narrative].

This land [on the north side of Demere Road] from the Waffle House all the way [west] to the Baptist church was owned by John Wells. He had a fifty-acre tract. He distributed it amongst his family, his chil'ren, and his sister. There's still some of that land left. I still own a piece of it.

I don't like to see all this land going away. Ain't nothing I can do about it. I don't like to see all this building going on the island.

This road here, Demere, used to be called Sea Island Road. In 1954, they built another road [paralleling Epworth east to Frederica Road] that goes to Sea Island. Then they named this road [from the Frederica River to McKinnon Airport] Demere Road.

The Military Road [built in 1736 or 1737] ran from Oglethorpe [Frederica] and went clean down here to Bloody Marsh. It was a shell road. There used to be a Hospital Road that crossed over from the Hilton and Dodge Mills to King's Way. There was another road down there they called Mary de Wan Road.[4] That road went right by St. Ignatius Episcopal Church, crossed the road [Demere], and cross Sea Palms clear on down to Retreat, Magnolia Street, and the pier.

There's a house at Retreat they call "the old tabby building" [or] "the Tabby House" [now a tourist shop]. There was a man by the name of Floyd White, a little small man. He was pretty near a hundred years old, and he stayed in that house. You know, it's an amazing thing—he was born in that building. It was his mama's house. He was a slave.[5]

I'll tell you some stories about him. He got a child, Liza, by Ellen Shepherd when he was about ninety-six years old. Liza just died last year [2005]. She was almost seventy years old. He used to drink corn liquor every day. He had a little still right there in his closet in the house. People were good about bringing him stuff. I guess someone brought him corn. He used to drink that corn liquor and walk the road. He wasn't drunk. He just drank that corn liquor. That's what held him up and made him live that long. He got killed by a car on Bloody Marsh curve in 1940. I believe he was buried out to the King Cemetery at Retreat.

The monument for Bloody Marsh used to be right by the road. They moved it back because someone come along there and poured red paint over it. They cleaned it off and moved it back from the road. Miss Parrish [Lydia Parrish, Maxfield Parrish's wife] owned Parrish Field back in there, back in Kelvin Grove. She recorded local singers there in a little house. She'd tape them and make recordings. I remember the Washboard Band. I knowed them good. They performed at the hotel on Sea Island and at festivals. They had a washboard, a trombone, a bugle, and drums. They was good.

I remember East Beach before it was developed. When I came here, there used to be a stream run out of the ocean that come out right by the Coast Guard place. Mr. Bruce owned that whole East Beach at one time. They named Bruce Drive after him. The causeway to East Beach used to have a little wooden bridge. They have a concrete bridge now.

They had a navy base here in World War II. That was before Glynco was even open. They unloaded barges with gas [at Gascoigne Bluff] for the planes and the cars. They used the King and Prince Hotel for the officers' club.

When I got here, the airport was where Redfern Village is. That was airport field, along by Longview Shopping Center. It run west to east. There wasn't much planes flying in and out of here.

Mr. Arthur True was good to me. I knowed him before he got married in 1937. Also, Mr. A. C. Oliver and Mr. Alfred Brockinton and Mr. Jim Edwards—Jerry, Buddy, Skippy Edwards. Those people were good to me. And Bubber Olsen and his father and all his sisters. We never had no race problems. We didn't have no intermarriage. Everybody knowed one another, and you could go anywhere you wanted to go. I knowed Jim Gould real well. I knowed his father. And Mr. Shadman and Clifford Postell and all the Taylors. Didn't have no trouble on this island. Didn't have no race problems.

Back in those days, blacks had a choice. They could go there [the Episcopal church in Jewtown] or to Christ Church [the Episcopal church near Frederica]. They was integrated. That's the way it was when I came here. You could go anywhere you wanted to go on the island back in those days. Everybody knowed one another. If a stranger come here, everybody would know it.

That's the way it was back on this island at that time. A beautiful place. Lot of woods. It's growing out of proportion. Too much. Too much. The island has changed 100 percent. It's getting crowded. There's too many people on the island. What they've done is, the poor people, they've taxed them off. Taxed them off until they couldn't stay. They had to sell or lose the land for taxes. It's been bad for the poor people. It's changing every day. It's still changing.

Sea Island does a good job at development, I must say. They do the very best in the world. Ain't nobody else can beat them. And they're good people. I've known them for more than seventy years. Sea Island owns 70 percent of all the undeveloped land on the island. The black and the white owns the other 30 percent. The only way to get some land is to get it from the people who have had it in the family for maybe 150 years.

They took the toll off the Brunswick–St. Simons Causeway. I wrote the governor, Sonny Perdue, asking him to leave it on. A lot of people ask me, say, "Why?" Well, I've been over here so long until I know it's getting crowded. We need another causeway because in case of a hurricane, people have to get off, and all the people couldn't get off. The toll wasn't all that much. Every year, I'd buy a sticker for thirty-five dollars. Two stickers—one for each car. I asked him to leave it on and make a study for another causeway—where it's going to leave the mainland and where it's going to land on St. Simons. Then build it and put a toll on it. When it's paid up, take the toll off of both causeways. Now, it costs a three-dollar toll to get on Jekyll but nothing to come over here, and people are crowding us out. So I asked him to leave it on and wrote him a nice letter. He wrote me back, wrote a nice letter back, and I appreciate that, too. He said that was his plan, to take it off. He said he appreciated the letter I wrote him. But we need another causeway because traffic that comes from the north end is bad. It's rough. On Demere Road, it's rough. And on the Sea Island Causeway, it's rough. It ain't going to get better. It's going to get worser all the time.

I don't leave the island when a hurricane comes. I stay right here on the island. I believe in God, and God is going to take care of me. I ain't worried about it. Like I asked the man, did he trust God? He said he ain't trusting God. He's going to get on off. I ain't never left. I stay right here. Me and my wife's family be the onliest ones to be here. When Dora came, I stayed right here. I didn't go nowhere. When Dora came, you could go down to the Frederica River and look across the marsh. It looked like an ocean going clean across to Brunswick.

I used to take out fishing parties and marsh-hen parties. Used to be, back in the marsh-hen season, we couldn't get enough guides to take people out. They came from all over the state of Georgia to hunt.

We'd fish on Frederica, Village, Hampton—all the rivers. Cusie Sullivan had a fishing camp down there. We'd rent a boat. There was another fishing camp called Taylor Fishing Camp and Priest Fishing Camp. The Taylor boys ran Taylor Fishing Camp. Priest Fishing Camp was up there by German Village. For entertainment, we had the Blue Inn on the south end of the island. It was a jazz club.

I ain't never seen nobody doing conjuring since I've been here. Some people might believe in roots and conjuring, but I don't believe in that kind of stuff. I believe in God. God is my personal savior, and I believe in Him. I go to St. Paul Baptist Church. I helped build it. I laid the bricks down there. We used to have an old wooden building. Long time. In 1970, we decided we wouldn't keep working on that old church. So we decided we'd just tear it down and build another church. So we just moved it over. Jasper Barnes was in charge of it. I laid the foundation and the bricks. But lately, they put a big annex back there behind it, an education building. I didn't build that.

Jasper Barnes lived up on Sugar Hill [across from Longview Shopping Center, behind the True Shopping Center]. I don't know why they called it Sugar Hill. Jasper built him a house there in the '60s. He's the onliest one on the island got a house with a basement all the way underneath it. Two or three bedrooms down there, just as dry as they can be. I done the brickwork. It's still there.

I knowed Bacchus Magwood real well.[6] When his house got burned down, I laid the foundation to build him another house. I think about what he used to tell me. He used to say, "To get somewhere, you have to give up something. You have to give up the good times, the fine clothes, fine shoes, fine women, the fine everything—to make it, to do what you can do." Bacchus lived right across from St. Paul Baptist on Demere. I think he came from Needwood on 17 [U.S. 17 near Howfyl Plantation north of Brunswick]. How it got its name, Needwood? There used to be a train run from Darien to Brunswick, and that's where the wood yard was at. When they get there, the steam would start going down in that old steam engine, and the conductor would tell the fireman, "We need wood."

I knowed Willis James Proctor and Enoch Proctor. Enoch was an interesting man. He worked some for Captain Brockinton. He was a World War I veteran. He was the onliest man who could swim over to Jekyll Island and swim back [see the Edwin Rubel Fendig, Jr.,

151

narrative]. Someone would tell him, "Can you swim to Jekyll?" He'd say, "That ain't no trouble." He'd jump in the water and pull his shoes off—he had a foot like a webfoot—and it wouldn't be long until he'd get over there. The onliest man ever known to do it. Seems like the first time he swimmed from over there, somebody carried him over there, and he said he was ready to leave. They told him they couldn't go then, so he come on back to St. Simons. He worked some for Captain Brockinton.

Julia Armstrong was Willis Proctor's sister. She had a bunch of chil'ren. Only one of them is living, and that's Pauline Burton. The Proctors were originally island people, far as I know. Been here for many years. They were South End. Black people owned all of that South End, all the way down to the pier where it came across where the baseball park is. Billy Small and Alvin Johnson and the Cummings, too. They owned all that property. There were acres and acres at Frederica that black people owned. I knowed Charles Wilson. He's the man who made baskets.[7] He was up at [the Harrington section of] Frederica.

We bought our groceries from Everett Groceries down to the village—Dutch Everett [see the James Dunn Gould III and Mary Frances Cannon Gould narrative]. You could go down there in the winter, and there wouldn't be nobody down there. All the people you'd see would be in the summer.

I've got some things I've got to do this year. This is 2006. It's got a six. I was born on the 6th of June, the sixth month of the year, in 1916. I've got to do it this year. My father was a doctor in the section where we was at. Anybody that get sick and their doctor say, "Ain't nothing we can do for them," they call my father. They said, "Call Uncle Jeff." My father would go in the woods and get them some medicine. Go in the woods and get it. I remember one time, a lady had a fever. She was burning up. Dr. Thomas said there wasn't nothing he could do. Said she'd die in bed the next morning. They said to get my father. My father went there. The next morning, the woman got up and walked around. He didn't say he was a doctor, but that was something he would do. And I know what he used.

There's so many things out there. God gives everybody something. He gives me something, gives you something. I don't care what you got, God gives him something in his head that maybe somebody else don't have.

But there's something out there to cure anything. Cure some kind of cancer. My daddy could take cataracts out your eyes without an operation. I ain't got no cataracts in my eyes. I know where all that stuff is. I can go get it. Now, blood comes from people and comes from animals. But there's blood right out there in them woods. If somebody in the settlement had low blood, my father could build the blood up. If they had high blood, he could bring that down. There's something out there in the woods. God put something here for everything, but you don't know what it is. My daddy could get that stuff and do it. My father could go out there and get it. My father could do it.

These are things I want to do, but I've got to do it this year. I don't know how long I got to live in this world, and I want to get this thing out before I die. Cure some kind of cancer, Alzheimer's. There's a heap of things I can do, but I've got to get it out this year. I can't wait until next year to get it out. I've got to get it done this year.

There's so many things that people don't understand. A tearpin [terrapin] is on a log, and it starts raining. As soon as it starts raining, he gets in the water to keep from getting wet. But he doesn't get in the water to keep from getting wet. He get off that log because he don't want that rain to be hitting on his back.

You take a pelican, a hawk, an eagle. They can just get up in the air and glide around out there with no type of wind. A pelican can fly just about a foot from the water against the wind. Nobody understands that. So God gives everybody something. He gives some knowledge. He didn't give it all to one man.

I might tell you another thing, too. The lawnmower was invented right down the street there in 1935 by Buster Bell. The onliest one living that knows about that is me and Bubber Olsen. He can tell you. He's the one that sold him the motor. Know what he [Buster Bell] done? He got him a car spring and sharpened it and put it down there at the bottom and made him a chassis wagon and pulled that wagon along and crank that thing up and cut grass. A man come along and say, "Hey, boy, what is that you got? I ain't never seen nothing like that before." Turned it over, bought it, went on and got a patent for it. The man gave him twenty-five dollars for it.

NOTES

1. William Anderson, *The Wild Man from Sugar Creek: The Political Career of Eugene Talmadge* (Baton Rouge: Louisiana State University Press, 1975), 207. The author notes that supporters would serve as "plants" to assure applause and laughter and to give the appearance that Talmadge support was scattered throughout the crowd, cueing Talmadge about things he wanted to speak on: "One prompter . . . asked, 'What about the Negroes going to our schools, Gene.' Talmadge responded, 'Before God, friend, the niggers will never go to a school which is white while I am governor.' "

2. Ibid., 22. Anderson writes, "Attesting to the complexity of the black-white relationship was the fact that Talmadge, an avowed segregationist, invited his black workers to eat lunch at his table in his home almost everyday during the farming season."

3. Edwin H. Ginn, *The First Hundred Years: A History of the American National Bank of Brunswick* (Brunswick, Ga.: Glover Printing Company, 1989), 52. Ginn writes that "the collapse of the economy couldn't have come at a worse time for the Cloister and the Sea Island Company. . . . Howard Coffin was badly crippled financially by the market Crash and was busy trying to salvage what he could. Wages were cut, and the hotel tried to get by with the minimum of help."

4. Don W. Farrant, *The Lure and Lore of the Golden Isles* (Nashville, Tenn.: Rutledge Hill Press, 1993), 73. Farrant writes, "One of the most cherished ghost stories of St. Simons Island is the saga of Mary the Wanderer (or, in Geechee dialect, 'Mary-de Wanda'). Many say they have seen her with her lantern held high, waiting and watching for the lover who went off to the mainland and never came back. . . . He shoved off in a rowboat, not knowing that hurricane-force winds were about to hit the islands. . . . She found his capsized boat. . . . Distraught with grief, she cast herself into the foaming waters. Some say Mary the Wanderer is still watching and waiting, especially on stormy nights."

5. Orrin Sage Wightman and Margaret Davis Cate, *Early Days of Coastal Georgia* (St. Simons Island, Ga.: Fort Frederica Association, 1955), 81. The authors note that "Floyd White . . . was born in this house and was the last Negro to live here. His mother, Victoria, was a slave of Retreat."

6. Ibid., 141. Wightman and Cate report, "Bacchus Magwood was an interesting person and made himself a good neighbor in the finest sense of the word. When Liddy who lived next door became ill, he took her to his house and cared for her until she died. Years later Bacchus' house burned and he was left homeless. A friend who inquired where he was staying was told, 'I move an' stay wid Lily.' 'Bacchus, I knew someone would give you a home for I remember when you took Liddy into your home and cared for her when she was sick and helpless.' Back came the reply, 'You cas' your bread!' "

7. Ibid., 157. Wightman and Cate describe Wilson's work: "Charles Wilson was the last of the old basket makers to ply his trade in this area. . . . To make his baskets Charles used the leaf stem of the cabbage palmetto, or sabal palm. He split these leaf stems and worked them to a uniform width and thickness with a pocket knife. As he wove these pieces into baskets he turned the outer surfaces of the stem to the outside so as to give the baskets a highly polished finish."

Olaf Helmer "Bubber" Olsen, Jr. and his sister Sonja

Olaf Helmer "Bubber" Olsen, Jr.

Olaf Olsen, Jr., is Sonja Olsen Kinard's older brother and a good friend of Buck Buchanan. He recounts how he and an ingenious black childhood friend, Buster Bell, built a gasoline-powered lawnmower years before they were commercially available.

Olsen recalls the rescue operation his father was involved in following the German U-boat sinking of two freighters off the Georgia coast in 1942. He also discusses his stints building Liberty ships and serving as a merchant marine during World War II.

I was born June 11, 1926, either at the hospital in Brunswick or on Gascoigne Bluff, St. Simons. My real name is Olaf Helmer Olsen, Jr. My grandmother's name was Helena. Helmer is the male for Helena. My sisters, instead of saying "brother," called me "Bubber." That's how I got that name.

Buster Bell and I used to play together when we were young. The Bells owned a lot of land in Jewtown. And Buster Bell used to cut yards. Well, I had a gas engine, and Buster said, "If I had that gas engine, I know something we can make." I said, "What's that?" He said, "I can find a way to cut grass."

This was about 1938, before gasoline lawnmowers. I was just about twelve years old at the time. Back then, the kids ten to twelve years old would cut yards for fifty cents with a sling blade. You'd work all day or two days for fifty cents. That's what Buster would do. He was a strong knocker. He was only about two years my senior.

So he got the motor from me. I also had a little metal lathe. And we took a block of oak wood and fixed it into a little child's wagon made out of wood with four wheels. He got a blade from one of those sling blades we used to cut yards. We put it on the end of a shaft and ran some pulleys to it. Buster would pull the wagon with the motor running, and it would cut the grass. But it would sling everything out in every direction. We never did get it really perfected. If it hit something, it would throw it out.

But he was the guy with the idea—just a kid. He had the wagon, and I had the engine. But it was basically the same thing as a lawnmower today. I don't know what happened to that mower. It's probably in back of their house falling apart.

His grandmother had one of the only stores in Jewtown, on the corner where you turn to go to Frederica Academy, on the opposite side of the road. I think the family still owns a good piece of land around there.

A car hit Buster about in the early 1940s, and he was in a nursing home for years until about five years ago, when he died.

I met Calvin Coolidge's wife by accident when I was six years old. They anchored their yacht across the river where Golden Isles Marina is now. People would anchor there and take a launch over to the Sea Island Yacht Club. When they came in, Daddy had everybody off of the dock, but I went on down there. I met her, not him.

John Life was one of the most respected black men on the island. He worked for my daddy back during the yacht club days, and he took care of me. He taught me to swim and row. He was a really good cook. Did a lot of barbecuing. There was George, Micy, John, and they had a sister. They owned all that property from Arnold Road north along Demere Road.

I remember when Buck Buchanan came to the island [see the Gloster Lewis "Buck" Buchanan narrative]. He married into the Wilson family. They owned a number of tracts in Jewtown. All of that used to belong to Hamilton Plantation.

I knew Captain Brockinton very well. He wanted me to be a harbor pilot, but I didn't want to. He owned a lot of land on the old Hamilton Plantation.

Back then, everybody used their names. You had Brady's Boat Yard, and Olsen's Yacht Yard, Spencer's, Wilson's, and so forth. Today, you don't do that. But there weren't many of us, and we knew each other personally. We worked together. If someone screwed us, we'd tell the other person to keep it from happening to him. Now, everything is owned by big corporations. It's an entirely different world.

We used to have one of the best harbors on the East Coast, back in the sailing-ship days. The sound then was about seventeen or eighteen feet deep in the shallowest place. A sailing ship's draft was only about thirteen or fourteen feet. They used to come to Darien on the Altamaha River through Doboy Sound, Brunswick and St. Simons through the St. Simons Sound, and the Satilla River through St. Andrew Sound. The pilot there was named Fader. The ships would unload ballast rocks and take on lumber. Sailing ships used

Olaf Helmer "Bubber" Olsen, Jr.

to go all the way up to Burnt Fort on the Satilla River for lumber.

During World War II, both the SS *Oklahoma* and the SS *Baton Rouge* were torpedoed about the same time and place. The Coast Guard sent out their patrol boat, which was a six-knot boat. They had to go all the way to the STS [St. Simons] sea buoy, about seventeen or eighteen miles offshore. Well, Daddy was a manager of the north end of Cumberland Island for the Candler family. There was a Civil Air Patrol at that time, and I believe it was Bob Ferguson who flew to Cumberland Island and dropped my daddy a note on a wrench asking him if he could assist. Could he go to the Sea Island Yacht Yard on St. Simons and pick up a doctor? So he got on Candler's boat and came in to gas up and pick up Dr. Avery. He went out what we call Portuguese Slough, which is right out in front of the King and Prince Hotel. He had a twenty-two-knot boat against a six-knot Coast Guard boat, and he had about half the distance that they went, so he got there first.

He picked up the lifeboats and had them in tow with some of the hurt sailors. The ones in bad shape, they put on his boat, and Dr. Avery tried to take care of them. I think a couple of them died on the way. So Daddy got in first with them. I was at the old St. Simons Coast Guard Station near the causeway when they came in. Someone tried to run me off, but I had to have my nose in everything.

They wanted to confiscate his boat to go back out there, but Daddy said, "Ain't nobody going to run this boat but me!" They put Daddy in the National Guard so that he could run the boat. He went on back out there that evening.

Edo Miller Funeral Home took charge of the dead seamen. The captain and the engineer from the *Baton Rouge* stayed at a hotel in Brunswick. They couldn't get a commercial boat to take them back and forth to the ship, and I was a young boy at that time, about sixteen, so Daddy said I could take them out in my thirty-five-foot balsa boat. I picked them up in Brunswick every morning at four-thirty and run them out to STS. There was a boat that picked them up at STS and took them on out to the ship. Then I'd be back in Brunswick in time for school. Every afternoon, I'd pick them up again and bring them back. That only lasted for three days. Every day, they'd bring me a present. The *Baton Rouge* life ring and the bell are now at the Coast Guard station museum on East Beach. I let the museum have them as a loan, so they can't get rid of them. Eventually, the ships were raised and brought into the St. Simons Sound.

Daddy would buy a boat and say it was mine. I had to keep the brass polished every day and all that stuff, but it was really his. But he'd call it mine so I would take care of it. Sort of tricky.

Daddy was assigned to the army unit—they always called it "the Georgia Navy"—in Brunswick. He got some of the wealthy men around here to join and furnish their boats. Candler had two boats. Frank Horn, who started the King and Prince Hotel, had a boat. Charlie King and Bob Furst were others. They hired captains and paid them out of their own pockets. I think there were six boats in all. They patrolled, and what they mainly did was to supply the islands—Cumberland, Sapelo, Jekyll—with soldiers and supplies.

There was a fighter pilot training facility on St. Simons. Occasionally, a plane would go down. I remember one of them was lost for a week between Little Cumberland Island and Cumberland Island. He went down in the marsh. Finally, they saw just a little bit of the plane's tail sticking up. The pilot was buried in mud. I believe the plane is still there.

People painted the top half of their car lights black to keep them from shining. That kept submarines offshore from seeing lights. The U-boat would sit on the inside of a buoy and wait, using its periscope. When a ship came by and moved between the buoy and the U-boat, it cut off the buoy's light. That's when the submarine would fire its torpedoes. Jack Lang interviewed the captain of that

U-boat in Germany a few years ago.[1]

I was one of the first employees at the shipyard where they built the Liberty ships. I was a runner. They didn't have telephones. So I went to work in the accounting department. There were only six of us there. I bet you the next day there must have been six hundred people, and a few days later three thousand people [were] working there. They were hiring them fast. When we started out, they gave me a pair of boots and a raincoat. Everything around there was like sludge. We had six runners, which was our communication system for a while, shuffling notes back and forth to everybody.

I ended up being a ship's fitter on the gunnel bar rail. I fitted pieces together and drilled holes on the gunnel bar rail. That was a rail they put in later because ships would break in half. It held them together. You ran an angle iron from one end to the other and riveted it in there. All we had to do was get it laid out. A crew of men would drill the holes, and a crew of men would rivet it.

After that, I joined the merchant marines and served mostly in the European theater during the war. We hauled everything from beer to guns and ammunition. Airplanes, gasoline, you name it. We had six or eight navy destroyers as escorts to protect us from U-boats. I was always lucky that we kept up with the convoy. If you dropped behind, you had trouble. There was a lead ship, with the escorts flanking us. Everybody in the convoy had to do ten knots. If you fell behind, you were on your own. We'd pick up a convoy coming from South America and go all the way up to the North Sea and go back down to the Mediterranean. But we wouldn't be in a convoy until we started out of the North Sea coming back down the United States coast again.

I loved going to sea. I'd be there today if it wasn't for marrying this girl I got. I married Gloria Lewis, from Rhode Island. I met her Christmas Eve night 1938. Every place that had something to do with our marriage is gone. We got married in St. James Lutheran

Church in Brunswick on Gloucester Street, had our reception at the Sea Island Yacht Club on St. Simons, spent the first night in the George Washington Hotel in Jacksonville. Everything is now gone.

St. Simons is being ruined. They should have never let them build the big condominiums they're putting up. The newcomers come in and want to drain the dollar out of everyone they can, then move on. They don't care about what happens to the land. All they care about is how much money can they make.

I would have never sold that property that the condos are on at the boatyard if the county hadn't messed me up and wouldn't let me build anything there. They told me all I could build was a single-family, single-story residence. Soon as I sold it, they [the buyers] went to town and got permits to build condos. They knew what they were doing when they bought it from me.

My daddy knew all of this was coming, and he tried to tell me. He said, "When the Yankees come here and find out we got better climate, and you can feel the four seasons, they're going to be coming out of Florida and the North and coming here. Everything from Daytona north to Charleston, they're going to start coming in and buying." This was about 1940-something. He said they'd get tired of that hot sun and start moving up this way.

He always told me to buy all the land I could, but I couldn't buy much.

NOTES

1. "German U-Boat Attack Off St. Simons Recalled," *Brunswick News*, December 7, 1996. The article states,

Reinhard Hardegen, captain of U-boat 123 . . . started his sinkings outside New York harbor in January 1942. As he worked his way down the coast, he sank two tankers off the coast of St.

Simons, the SS *Oklahoma* and the SS *Esso Baton Rouge*, on April 8, 1942. . . . A total of 24 seamen were killed on the two tankers and all but five were identified and shipped to their hometowns for burial. The five unidentified (badly burned) were buried in separate graves in Palmetto Cemetery in Brunswick with metal markers reading "Unknown Seaman—1942" . . . via the arrangements of Sonja [Olsen Kinard]. Brunswick native Jack Lang interviewed Captain Reinhard Hardegen at his home in Bremen, Germany. . . . This meeting with the 83-year-old robust, former U-boat captain proved to be very interesting. His recall of the war was vivid, including his sinkings of the two ships off St. Simons Island. In the interview, Captain Hardegen emphasized that he was a German U-boat captain, not a Nazi. Hardegen had the distinction of being honored by both Germany and the United States. First, after his initial successful sinkings . . . Hitler gave him the Iron Cross with oak leaf clusters at a private banquet. In a documented account of this event, Hitler asked Hardegen how he thought the war was going for Germany. The brash 28-year-old captain answered to the effect, "I think you should build more U-boats and less tanks and not look towards the East (Russia)." A red-faced Hitler shot back, "Young man, you don't know what you're talking about." Secondly, in 1990, Hardegen and his wife were brought to Jacksonville, Fla., and honored for his gesture of saving lives when a tanker ablaze from a torpedo hit from Hardegen's sub had to be shelled by deck guns to effect sinking. Noticing the people on the Jacksonville Beach, Hardegen maneuvered his U-boat, at the risk to his crew, between the shore and the ship to fire. This avoided his shells over-shooting the tanker and hitting into the large crowd gathered on shore to watch the spectacle. Amusingly, Hardegen told Lang about an incident. . . . He said a lady had refused to shake his hand and termed him "still the enemy." In the next breath, she added, "I don't shake hands with Yankees either." This puzzled Hardegen as he considered all Americans Yankees. . . . His parting words to Lang were: "Enemies yesterday—friends today."

Sara Evelyn Blackwell Oliver and A. C. Oliver, 1940s

Sara Evelyn Blackwell Oliver

Perhaps more than any other resident of St. Simons, Mrs. Oliver exemplifies the battle between old island charm and new development. Her home, now surrounded by large condominium structures, sits on historic ground overlooking St. Simons Sound, land that was once the site of another battle.

In 1735, James Oglethorpe established Delegal's Fort on the south end of St. Simons, where Mrs. Oliver's home is situated. Any ship entering the harbor had to pass the fort's thirteen-cannon battery. By 1739, the enlarged and renamed Fort St. Simons "presented the appearance of a neat village, with streets regularly laid off, and with more than one hundred clapboard houses occupied by the soldiers and their families."[1] A Spanish invasion of thirty-four ships, led by Florida's governor, Don Manuel de Montiano, successfully ran Oglethorpe's gauntlet of fire the afternoon of July 5, 1742, and eventually captured the fort. Unlike Fort Frederica, now a national park, the Fort St. Simons site, which represents Spain's last hold on land north of Florida, is commemorated only by several historical markers.

Mrs. Oliver's husband, A. C., built many homes on the island. Through his work, Mrs. Oliver has firsthand knowledge of homebuilding on St. Simons.

She recalls their 1964 encounter with Hurricane Dora, which demolished a row of nearby beach cottages. President Lyndon B. Johnson visited the area soon after to inspect the damage. She recalls his motorcade parked behind her house.

Mrs. Oliver passed away three months after sharing her thoughts and memories.

I'm originally from Shady Dale, which is in Jasper County, Georgia, near Madison. It's beautiful country. I was born in our house on August 16, 1915, in a section called Hopewell-Blackwell settlement, right out of Monticello. You go out of Monticello into Shady Dale and Madison. There wasn't a hospital any closer than Macon. There were three children—two boys and me. One of the boys died when he was a year and a half. We grew up without any money to speak of. You existed. You farmed, and you existed with what you made. The first time I saw the ocean was when I started teaching school.

My husband, Arthur Cloud Oliver, was from Sylvania, which is in Screven County near the Savannah River. He was born in 1914. A. C. was working for Robert & Company in Atlanta. They had the contract to start Glynco, the navy base [in Brunswick].

Sara Evelyn Blackwell Oliver, 2002

They sent him down to locate the boundaries for the base, where the railroads should go, that sort of thing. He had been working on railroads with Robert & Company at the general depot in Conley, up near Jonesboro. He worked in and out of the area for Mr. Harold J. Friedman, who was a county engineer, and A. C. had worked with the coastal geodesic survey in establishing all the elevation points in the area.

After he did that, A. C. was called back to Atlanta because Robert & Company got the contract to build the Bell [B-29] bomber plant [now Lockheed Martin] in Marietta. But when he got back up there, he decided he didn't want to do that. He wanted to come back down here. For one reason, A. C.'s mother and father and brother lived on St. Simons at that time. The Olivers' house was Cedar Point, on the corner of Fourth and Beachview Drive. That land is still there. The house has been demolished. His brother worked at the pulp mill in Brunswick as an engineer.

My husband was a licensed surveyor. A. C. went to Georgia Tech for one year, but he did not get a degree. Everything he learned, he learned on the job. He'd been with a crew that surveyed the Okefenokee Swamp, laying out landlines for the highway department. They came across snakes, hogs, alligators, you name it. They all loved it. Just loved it.

Before we married, we knew each other because his brother married a friend I had roomed with when we were teaching school in Butler, Georgia. I taught grammar school and high school. Then I went to work for the Georgia Power Company in Atlanta. We came to St. Simons in 1942 and built this house in 1950. All the houses had beautiful lawns out to the high-water mark. This land used to be a wooded area where people picnicked and children played and climbed trees and made tree houses. There were paths all through this area. There were cassina bushes that had grown up, and all sorts of myrtle. Everybody thought this was just a public park, and nobody had ever tried to buy the land. The newspaper family, the Leavys, owned this land at that time.

There were houses across Ocean Boulevard. The Doyle house was there. And Grady Doster built a house next to the Baptist church the same time we built our house. This house sits on what used to be Fort St. Simons, which General Oglethorpe erected. But we have never found anything from that era.

We moved here from Atlanta right after the merchant ships were torpedoed. We came down here one weekend when they were bringing them in [see the Allen Augustine Burns, Jr., narrative and the Olaf Helmer "Bubber" Olsen, Jr., narrative]. They were anchored right out here [in St. Simons Sound]. You could see the damage. There was always that danger of being invaded. That danger was always lurking. We had to have blackout curtains on everything.

During World War II, the navy planes were in and out all of the time. All the boats made so much noise. When one, a PT boat, went out, you knew one was going out. I thought it was the worst thing in the world when they tore those wonderful blimp hangars down.

When we came here in 1942, the ocean was lapping at the door of the Coast Guard station at East Beach. We looked at a house on Third Street on East Beach and seriously considered buying it, but the water came right up to the door. Now, there are several hundred yards of land between there and the ocean. It's just absolutely amazing that all of that land is now built out. The King and Prince Hotel once had a big lawn out in front of it. But the ocean water kept coming in. During the war, the water kept coming in, and the navy put a concrete sea wall in front of the hotel.

The first house A. C. owned here was on the corner of Mallory and Magnolia. Two men from Sandersville—one was a Coca-Cola bottler—had built those little stucco houses on Mallory, near Mallory Park. Incidentally, there was an Indian burial ground that was discovered there back in the 1960s.

I always wanted to live on the water. As soon as A. C. could find a place, we moved to Beachview Drive. We built that one. By that time, the water was coming in. We couldn't afford to put in bulkheads, so we sold it and bought this piece of land and moved in here. The Culvers and Deloaches moved in next to us several years later. A. C. built the Deloach house from scratch. The Culver house—there was a small house there, and they added onto that older house. Betty [her daughter] was three years old when we moved into this house. Chuck [her oldest son] was seven.

I keep my downstairs windows open all summer. Upstairs is air-conditioned. Downstairs is not. I pull them up in summertime, and they stay up. The moisture isn't good for furniture, though.

When we first came here, you drove down to the fort [Frederica], before the federal government had it. Just get out and wander around. Everybody did on Sunday afternoon, if you wanted to drive someplace. The Stevens family lived right down there. The Dodge Home was right there [see the James Dunn Gould III and Mary Frances Cannon Gould narrative and the Sarah "Sally" Elizabeth Taylor Jones and Dr. Charles E. Pearson narrative].

There weren't many street names on St. Simons back then, unless it was named for somebody who lived on that street. If someone needed to know where somebody lived, you had to tell them they lived near Mr. so-and-so. Mary Everett was the postmistress in the village. She knew everything, where everyone was.

Beachview Drive was called Railroad Avenue because there once had been a small horse-drawn rail connecting the pier with a hotel at Massengale Park. Most of that road has washed away and is covered by ocean. It would have been a couple of blocks past [east of] where the Johnson Rocks are now.

We were here when Hurricane Dora struck. We crossed the street and stayed overnight in the First Baptist Church's fellowship hall. I had a key. I was in charge of the kitchen at the time. It was just A. C. and me. At that time, we didn't have designated hurricane shelters. The police would stop in every once in a while and tell us what was happening. We didn't really sleep that night. The Bolands—Rosa, Vickie, and David—stayed in their house across the street from ours. They were right close to where the block of homes washed away. They had no idea until morning that those four or five houses behind them had been demolished. Evidently, the hurricane spawned a tornado, which hit those homes.

We had just put new wall-to-wall carpeting in the living room. Only about two drops of water came in under the front door. But there was debris all over the yard—sand and rocks. We didn't know what to think when we saw those summer cottages washed out. We were just thankful we weren't among those that had been demolished.

After that, a couple of days later, President Johnson came to the island to inspect the damage. We began hearing that he was coming. We had no idea he would show up at our back door. They parked right on the corner on the other side of the street behind our house [at the corner of Oglethorpe Avenue and Seventh Street].[2] They had sent equipment to clear the roads so that the entourage could get in with cars. There were a number of cars because every one of the congressmen who could come came with him. I don't remember who they were, but I remember there were lots of people who came with him. He got out and walked around and looked, but they didn't stay very long. Everybody in the neighborhood came over and tried to see what was going on. We were just standing around, mouths wide open, trying to absorb whatever there was to see.

The president immediately afterward said that a sea wall was needed, and pretty soon a wall was being built. I didn't realize at the time that there are rock quarries up near Macon, which is where I believe the sea-wall rocks came from. They call them "the Johnson Rocks" because the president ordered the wall to be built.

We bought the two lots across the street by the beach for about six thousand dollars just before Hurricane Dora struck. Those two lots now are taxed for several million dollars. We have riparian rights all the way to the low-water mark. You lose or gain land as the shoreline shifts. Some people still pay taxes on underwater property, which amounts to about a dollar a year. But because of the depth of the ships' channel, and as long as that ships' channel is maintained, the land will never fill back.

I've never been afraid of hurricanes, no more than anyone else. I didn't think I'd ever leave until I heard about New Orleans and the aftereffect of Hurricane Katrina—not the hurricane itself, but what happened after. No lights, no water, no anything else. Because of all that, I would leave now. Until New Orleans came along, I would not have said I would leave.

My husband sort of backed into building houses. After World War II, the county started laying water and sewer lines because there had never been any of either on the island. A. C. became associated with Bob Perrott, a Dr. Pepper bottler, who had some lots behind what is now the Sweet Mama's and the Crab Trap. He asked A. C. to build some houses for him. After a while, he got his contractor's license. A. C. developed the River View neighborhood on the other side of Longview.

Mr. Perrott started the 10-2-4 Ranch on the east side of Frederica Road [across from the St. Clair subdivision]. There used to be a little stable there where the Perrotts kept their horses. A. C. was in charge of clearing that land, which was full of rattlesnakes. Somebody told him to get some goats, and the goats would get rid of the snakes. So we went to Sterling and got a bunch of goats and drove them back in our coupe, which had a big trunk in the back. Sure enough, the goats got rid of the snakes.

Rosa Boland's father was a Vickers. They had relatives near Tifton. A man named Abbott built a lot of the houses over here down on Ocean Boulevard. A lot of those houses had to have been built in the early 1930s. Mr. J. C. Strother, who owned Strother's Hardware Store in the village, developed Oglethorpe Park [see the Joseph Albert Bruce Faircloth, Jr., and Jane Lou McLeod Faircloth narrative]. The houses were sold for around sixty-five hundred or seventy-five hundred dollars. Around the same time, Mr. Brice, a wholesale grocer from Vidalia, had bought that King's Terrace land behind the Presbyterian church and started that neighborhood.

There used to be some characters on the island. There was a man named Youngblood. Everyone called him "Blood." A great big man. He was sort of a half-wit. He wasn't really crazy or dangerous to anybody. He lived in a tree down in the village. Everybody knew him. He had no home. He slept in one of those old gnarled cedar trees down in the village in Neptune Park.

There was another man named Mousy. He peddled parched peanuts. He was always down in the village with these little bags of peanuts.

Mr. Gramling was a surveyor. When I first saw Mr. Gramling, I thought I'd never seen anybody in the world with as many wrinkles or look so old. Mrs. Gramling was kin to everybody. All the other surveyors could never tie most of Mr. Gramling's surveying points in with the other points. They declared that everything Mr. Gramling did, they didn't know how or why he did it.

It's been a wonderful area to live in. Just a wonderful area.

NOTES

1. Orrin Sage Wightman and Margaret Davis Cate, *Early Days of Coastal Georgia* (St. Simons Island, Ga.: Fort Frederica Association, 1955), 27.

2. Duane Riner, *Brunswick News*, September 12, 1964. The paper reports, "President Johnson took a whirlwind automobile tour of Brunswick and St.

Simons Island yesterday, stopping twice along the route, and concluded his 90-minute visit with assurance that the federal government 'will be in here to lend every possible assistance'. . . . His second exit from the limousine . . . occurred at the foot of Seventh Street on St. Simons Island where beach cottages had been undermined and destroyed by the pounding surf."

Edwin Rubel Fendig, Jr.

Edwin Fendig, Jr., is a longtime harbor pilot for the port of Brunswick, Georgia. In this narrative, he talks about the transition of St. Simons from a summer vacation destination for mainlanders to a full-time place of residence.

He recalls in detail the 1972 tragedy in which ten people died after a ship struck the Sidney Lanier Bridge. The account of the accident in the New York Times *states that "the 11,000-ton vessel,* African Neptune, *making her way down river bound for the sea, slammed into the mile-long Sidney Lanier Bridge and destroyed a three-span, 450-foot section. Cars and trucks waiting on the bridge for the ship to pass fell into the river amid tons of shattered concrete and twisted steel girders."[1]*

Twice drafted into the military, Fendig recounts his World War II experiences. He also remembers an interesting local man who island-hopped from St. Simons to Sapelo Island to visit his girlfriend.

I was born June 27, 1927, in the old hospital on the south end of Brunswick. My father, Edwin Rubel Fendig, Sr., was a native Brunswickian. His father was from Indiana and was president of the First National Bank in Brunswick. In that bank, there is a picture of him, and every time I walk in there I get shivers because it looks like he's looking right at me. My grandfather's best friend was named Edwin Rubel, and that's where my father's name came from.

My mother came from Washington, Georgia, in Wilkes County. She was a country girl. She had never been out of Wilkes County until she graduated from high school. She went to an eleven-grade school at that time. Then she went to the Georgia State College for Women in Milledgeville. At that time, she could get a teacher's certificate in two years. Her first teaching job was in Darien, Georgia. Then she came and taught senior English at Glynn Academy High School in Brunswick sometime in the early 1920s. She met Dad here, and they got married in 1925. His father gave my dad the property right next to where we live now on Virginia Street. They built their house and moved into it in 1928.

Back then, St. Simons was occupied primarily by Brunswickians during the summertime. The causeway connecting Brunswick and St. Simons was already built, in 1924. They came over here after school let out in June. When school started back up after Labor Day, they'd move back to Brunswick. But my mother was taken with this place. So when my dad said, "Okay. It's time to pack up and go back to Brunswick," she waved good-bye. She didn't want to leave the island. They never went back to Brunswick.

I went to Sidney Lanier Elementary School in Brunswick for the first six grades. My first-grade teacher was Miss Stallings. We had great high-school teachers at Glynn Academy. Miss Jane Macon was one of them. She taught my dad English. There was also

Edwin Rubel Fendig, Jr., 2005

Miss Bunkley and Miss Tracy, who taught trigonometry. We didn't take any entrance exams for college then. I remember going to the registrar's office at the University of Georgia. He said, "Where did you go to high school?" I told him, and he said, "I'm wasting time talking to you. Come right on in."

I had been in the Boy Scouts and learned signaling. I could semaphore, and I knew Morse code. I could signal with a light because there was a lot of naval activity around St. Simons during World War II. Boats would come into the sound and anchor, and I'd see them talking to the Coast Guard station by the lighthouse. That particular station was just a little hut they set up as an HEIP [Harbor Entrance Identification Post]. During the war, they had an entrance signal of the day. Every boat—navy, shrimp boat, or whatever—had to know the signal, and you had to broadcast it to that station when you entered the harbor. If you didn't know the signal, they'd send a boat from the Coast Guard station on the Frederica River, which would come out and inspect you.

Signalmen like to talk, and there were a lot of navy vessels anchored in the harbor. At night, you could see them chatter. Just shooting the bull. I learned to signal with a flashlight so I could talk to the ships when they'd come in. One time, a ship came in and anchored, and I flashed him and started talking to him. The man signaled back and said, "We want to come over to the pier. Can we get permission from you to use your pier?" I signaled back that it wasn't my pier, "but you can come on over." And they came on in on a small boat.

We'd go to the Coast Guard station on East Beach and help them stand watch up in that watchtower. You could hear explosives going off all the time with the blimps [hunting U-boats] and all the navy activity.

A Coast Guard auxiliary formed here. The Coast Guard needed help patrolling the area. Mr. Olsen, who lived on the island, was involved with the military more than anyone else on the shore. He used to take the navy out on Mr. Candler's yacht. His son Bubber Olsen shared a lot in that work, too [see the Olaf Helmer "Bubber" Olsen, Jr., narrative].

I graduated from high school on June 1, 1945, a Friday night. The next day, on Saturday, my dad took me to Jacksonville, and I was sworn into the navy. On Sunday, I was eighteen years old. That was a big weekend for me. The war was over in Europe, but the war was still on with Japan. At that time, we were still planning to invade Japan. They estimated we would lose one million men. I was gung-ho to go.

My first assignment after boot camp was to report to a ship in Norfolk, Virginia. We didn't know where we were going. There were so many of us on that ship, we had to sleep on the deck. We went through the Panama Canal and bumped the bottom. On the Balboa side—the western side of the canal—the skipper dropped anchor, and we sat there for about a couple of weeks. They were sending us to the Philippines, which was the staging area for invasion. It was full of soldiers and sailors. I probably wouldn't be here talking today if Mr. Truman hadn't dropped that bomb when he did. We were right there ready to go.

The war ended during the time I was on that ship. They finally picked up anchor, and we sailed into San Francisco Bay. At that moment, Admiral Halsey was returning from the Pacific with his fleet. These people had been out there for the whole war, and we came in with them—straight out of boot camp—to receive the salute from the people of San Francisco. People came out any way they could to celebrate their return. I can't explain what it was like. The harbor was full of boats and yachts, giving the flotilla a big reception, and they thought we were a part of Halsey's fleet.

My first duty when I got to the Philippines was to go into the jungle and stand guard on an ammunition dump. There were still

Edwin Rubel Fendig, Jr., at the helm of a pilot boat, 2005

Japanese out there who didn't know the war was over. They found some navy boys there hung up by their feet with their throats cut. I was eighteen years old, and I had a carbine. If I heard something out in that jungle, man, I just cut loose with the gun. I don't mind telling you, I was scared.

I graduated from the University of Georgia in 1950. When I came back home, Bill Way was organizing an Air National Guard unit in Brunswick. He had to have so many men before they were officially recognized as a guard unit. At the time, I was in the Navy Reserve. He told me, "I need your help. I need you to be sworn into the Air National Guard." I said, "I'm in the Navy Reserve. I'll have to get out of that to be in the National Guard." But he talked me into helping him get his unit organized. Next thing I know, I'm getting sworn in as a private first class in the bottom of the Oglethorpe Hotel in Brunswick. If you'll remember, in June of 1950, the Korean War started. We hadn't been sworn in two or three days, and we got frozen. They activated that unit in January 1951. I had majored in personnel management, so they made me a personnel officer.

There were a number of interesting people on the island when I was growing up. Enoch Proctor was a very unusual fellow. He was one of the island Proctors, whom Proctor Lane is named for. Enoch was strong. He could pick up anything you asked him to. When people used to drive their cars on the beach, occasionally someone would get stuck in the sand. Enoch was our local wrecker man. He could pick up the back of a car so someone could put something underneath the tires. I never saw that, but that was his reputation. He never said much. He'd acknowledge you with a grunt. He would collect clams for people. I've seen him go out with an empty croaker sack and come back with it full of clams. He'd get them on the marsh side of Gould's Inlet.

Enoch used to work as a deck hand for the harbor pilot, Captain Brockinton, when they used a sailing vessel. The sailing vessel would stay way offshore, and the pilots would stay on it seven days a week. They never knew when a ship might come in, so they stayed out there. Captain Brockinton used to say he ate fish twenty-one times a week. They'd come by boat to the pier for supplies or to change crews.

Anyway, Enoch had a girlfriend on Sapelo Island. Sometimes, he'd jump out of the pilot boat off the St. Simons beach and swim ashore. Then he'd walk down to East Beach and wade across to Sea Island. He'd walk the length of Sea Island and go across Little St. Simons and Egg Island. From Egg Island, he'd swim to Sapelo. He had to time his crossing from Egg Island to Sapelo with the tide, probably at slack tide.

Mr. Strachan, who owned a house by the pier, used to hire fellows to drag a seine net out on the beach in front of his house. That's where the pilot boat used to anchor, and it's where Enoch would jump off and come ashore. So one day, it may have been at dark, Enoch comes ashore and got caught up in that net. When those men pulled that net on the beach, Enoch comes walking out of it. Mr. Strachan never saw those fellows again! Enoch died in the '60s when he was probably in his seventies or eighties.

There was another fellow, an interesting character named Cy. His last name was Youngblood. He worked for J. C. Strother. The old Casino building, where the library is now, used to have a bowling alley. Cy used to set the pins. He'd stay right there at the end of the lane setting up pins, no matter how many were flying around.

My mother shot sixteen-millimeter film of the 1936 dedication of the Coast Guard station on East Beach. When people say that the beach is washing away, you need a baseline to go on. In 1936, the high-tide mark was at the steps of the Coast Guard station. If you go look at the Coast Guard station now, there's more than a hundred yards of land built up before you get to the beach.

I also have a sixteen-millimeter movie my mother took of Paul

Redfern when he took off from Sea Island to Brazil [see the Eleanor Stiles Cate narrative and the James Dunn Gould III and Mary Frances Young Gould narrative].

I was raised on Virginia Street, which is part of King City, the oldest planned neighborhood on St. Simons [see the John Spencer Harrison "Harry" Aiken, Jr., narrative]. It's named after the King family, who owned Retreat Plantation. Captain Alfred Brockinton lived just down the street, and he's the reason I became a harbor pilot for the city of Brunswick. He was a contractor and a harbor pilot, and his daddy and his grandfather were harbor pilots. But when he came along, there was very little pilot business going on. His dad and grandfather worked on sailing vessels. They go back to the sailing-ship days. They would guide boats into the East River of Brunswick and to Gascoigne Bluff on the Frederica River here on St. Simons, where the old logging mill was. The ships used to load lumber right there. Most of the rivers on the coast of Georgia at one time or another experienced sailing vessels coming in to load cargo.

I'll tell you how piloting came about. It followed what they did over in Europe. In the old days, there was no way to communicate with the shore. You had ships that came in here, which was primarily a British colony, and the ships were primarily British. For years, the Brits ruled the seas. Some of the ship owners had sense enough to make the captain part owner of the ship. So he had a vested interest in getting that ship moving and safely to port. In those days, time wasn't of the essence like it is today. There was no communication and no aids to navigation. No markers or buoys. You got there when you got there.

When a captain got to a harbor, he would put a man up on the bow and lead-line his way in. They would throw the line and read the depth. So you would have to feel your way in. Then, when you got to port, you saw a fellow over there about to go out. And that captain might have been sitting there in port for two months. You have to remember, in those days, those captains and crew might be away at sea for three or four years. The captain leaving might say, "You just found your way in. Come with me and help me find my way out." So the captain who just came in would take a little boat to pull behind the outgoing vessel, and he'd show the other captain how to get out. The other captain would say, "You know, I owe you something for that." You know what he paid with? He'd pay in gold.

Maybe while he's out there, here comes another captain on a boat who'd never been there before. The first captain says to himself, "You know, I don't have to be gone for three or four years. I can stay here on the shore, bring my family over here, and take these fellows in and out." So that's what he did.

Then another fellow sees this and says to himself, "I'm going to do the same thing. I'm going to help ships in and out of this port. But I'm going to go offshore. The next time a boat shows up, I'm going to bring it in."

The original pilot says to himself, "This fellow is cutting into my turf." So he goes and gets a faster boat to beat the other pilot out there.

Both of them try to be the first one to "speak the vessel." Whoever spoke the vessel first got the business. One pilot might sight a sail near Sapelo Island and go after it. Finally, these two fellows would say, "Let's stop fighting over these boats. You take one, and I'll take the next one. We'll just split what we make." And that was the beginning of piloting.

When I was growing up, there was only one harbor pilot for Brunswick. That was Captain Brockinton. He knew me since I was born, and he knew I was interested in boats. He had two daughters. Had one of them been a boy, he would have become the harbor pilot instead of me. At that time, women weren't accepted as pilots. They are now, but not then. He had several nephews who worked with him, but none of them worked out for one reason or another. He needed some help one day, and he said, "Come on. I need you to take me out to a ship." I never had run his boat before, but I took him out and put him on a ship. This was in the 1950s.

So I started working with him. I kept the boat in working order and took him out and put him on all of the ships. Finally, I was recognized as an official apprentice, and my time was applied towards being a pilot, which took about six years. I remember bringing my first boat in. I was thirty-something, and I was ready to go.

Captain Brockinton always talked about the *Great Eastern*. She was an actual ship—a big ship. He would frequently refer to her when some captain would come in with a small ship and anchor way offshore. We'd have to go out twenty miles to get them. And he'd say, "That captain must think he's got the *Great Eastern*." But when I got my harbor pilot's license, I was ready for the *Great Eastern*.

Herman Talmadge was the governor of Georgia when they started building the Sidney Lanier Bridge in Brunswick, and he stopped it. You can go back and check that. Glynn County never voted for a Talmadge, neither Gene or Herman. The county had always voted Republican. My daddy was a big supporter of Gene Talmadge. In fact, Gene Talmadge appointed Daddy an admiral in the Georgia Navy, which is an honorary appointment. My dad went and got a uniform, and every time Gene Talmadge was in this area, he would put that uniform on. He took Gene Talmadge all around and introduced him to people that he knew. Incidentally, and without knowing about my father, Governor Barnes later appointed me an admiral in the Georgia Navy, too.

The Sidney Lanier Bridge was built about 1956. Now, the *African Neptune* came in here from Panama to get paper and maybe some cargo from Hercules [Powder Company]. They sailed in here one afternoon and left the next night at about nine o'clock. It was an American flagship with an American crew. The ones I dealt with were U.S. citizens.

When we went out that night, we had a little trouble getting away from the dock.[2] I had to do a good bit of maneuvering. At that time, we just had small tugs in port. Not all pilots do the docking work. We did. Some ports have docking pilots that come about from the tugboats. But Brunswick, being a smaller port, there wasn't enough business for a docking pilot to do the work. So we've always done it. Every pilot has had some problems docking ships. I've heard it said that until a pilot bends some steel, they're not a real pilot.

The night the *African Neptune* ran into the Sidney Lanier Bridge [November 7, 1972], one of the hardest things for me to accept was that I was doing the best that I could possibly do, and it wasn't good enough. I had to depend upon someone else, and someone else didn't do what he was supposed to do. We were approaching the bridge, and the quartermaster turned the wheel the opposite direction from the instructions I gave him.[3] It's unbelievable how many times that has happened—not in that situation, and not with the same consequences. The mate is responsible to see that the quartermaster turns the wheel the way that the pilot tells him to turn it. We were already going left ten. I said, "Left twenty." I wanted a little more wheel on it.

The next thing I knew, the bow sort of swerved to starboard. I looked up at the rudder indicator. When the ship got written up after this accident, they determined it was not convenient for the pilot to navigate and see the rudder indicator. The quartermaster has to look at it, and the mate has to look at it. It was night, but I saw where we were going. When I saw us swerve that way, I knew that the rudder was going right twenty. We were going exactly the opposite direction.

It was a sickening feeling. A terrible feeling. The ship was almost at the bridge. I'll never forget. And she almost stopped. The ship was jumping up and down because we dropped both anchors, and all the power we had was going to stern. If we had another minute of time, she wouldn't have touched the bridge. The way that bridge was built, the concrete decking was sitting on top of the piling, and the cars were right there over the piling. There was nothing to hold the stability of that piling. She barely touched it. The ship barely touched that concrete deck and pushed it right on over. I remember bracing myself, but we didn't even feel it on the ship.[4]

We took the *African Neptune* back to the dock that night. I took that ship out the next day. They took the quartermaster's license. The ship had a ship's recorder on it, thank goodness, which proved that had he not taken that right turn, it would have gone left. The captain backed me up. So did the mate. And Lawrence Gray, the other harbor pilot at the time, happened to be on the ship. The new Sidney Lanier Bridge has a lot more room now. With that bridge, we only had a maximum of 250 feet from steel to steel. With the new one, we have over 1,000 feet.

In 1964, Captain Brockinton wrote to the local pilot commission, with a copy to the department of transportation in Atlanta, recommending that they move the traffic barricades on the bridge further back. The barricades were right there at the opening to the bridge where the span was. He wrote, "One day, that bridge is going to be struck. Please move the guards back to at least keep the people off the area where it will likely be hit." Do you think they did that? They didn't do it until after the accident. I got a copy of that letter. After the *African Neptune* accident, they moved the barricades halfway down the bridge.[5]

In an accident like that, the value of the ship plus its cargo is available to compensate for what the people suffered, the survivors' claims. The lawyers representing the survivors tried to prove that the ship was not seaworthy. If they could prove that, they could go after the entire fleet. And they did. But when the lawyers for the ship owner, Farrell Lines, appealed it to the federal court in New Orleans, the court ruled that the ship owner was only liable for the one ship. I don't know what the total settlement was. The Coast Guard took months confirming what I told them, but I knew exactly what happened.

Today, each ship has an agent onshore who represents that ship. We take our orders from the agent. He'll say, "Pick my ship up at such-and-such a time and bring it to such-and-such a dock." And we'll be there. There are six harbor pilots in Brunswick now. Lawrence Gray has been one for a number of decades. We get a schedule with tentative ship arrival dates and get updates as the time gets closer. If a ship hits weather, it could slow it down. Sometimes, we don't know where it is until it's within radio-hailing distance. We have a big antenna that lets us talk to a ship about thirty or forty miles away. They'll call us on the radio to be sure we do know when they approach.

The Third World countries don't require their captains to speak English. But they can usually speak enough English for us to communicate. If they can't understand what you're saying in numbers, like on a compass, you can write it down or point to something. We also give rudder commands like "Five degrees to the right." Thirty-five degrees is hard-over. After you reach thirty-five degrees, the rudder's no good. You can communicate anywhere between zero and hard-over to make a turn. You can also point at your rudder indicator. If they can't understand what you're saying, you can point to ten on your right side, ten on your left, and so on. That's a minimum. You've got to be able to do that to bring a ship in.

We have two pilot boats now which were made in Seattle and hauled here by truck. We own our own boats and do more than just guide ships in and out of port. Our boats have special equipment that let us make soundings of docks and the harbor and the channels here or elsewhere, and produce it just like the Corps of Engineers. We have contracts that call for us to make regular soundings. We had to build these boats to do more than just docking work.

We are licensed by the state. Each state in the union that has ports has its own laws covering the pilots in those states' waters. Under Georgia law, they authorize the city to appoint a Brunswick Pilot Commission that sets the rates that we can charge shipping companies and are responsible to seeing that a service is available for these ships that want to come in.

What happened back in those early days is those two fellows who piloted ships in said, "You know, we've got us a good deal. Let's raise our prices some." And they did. The first thing the captain wants to know is, "How much are you going to charge me to take me in there? Maybe I can get into port myself." Some captains would say, "No. You're charging too much. I'm not going to pay you. I'll go up to Savannah or down to Jacksonville." So the people on the shore get worried about it and say to the pilots, "Wait, you're taking business away from us. We're going to see that your rate is competitive." And they formed a local pilot commission.

The rates are based on a ship's tonnage and draft—so much a foot. The closer she gets to the bottom, the more it costs her. There is a charge to get a ship in and another charge to get her out. Other ports have other methods of charging ships. But the rates are competitive. For example, Brunswick likes to be a little under Savannah and Jacksonville. As we've gotten bigger and more expensive to operate, our rates are closing that gap.

Right now [in 2005], we are averaging about thirty-five or forty ships a month, which is about one a day. Back in the 1970s, Lawrence Gray and I were doing twelve or fifteen ships a month. The dangerous part is getting on and off the ships. Most pilots get on and off a ship on a rope ladder. Some of the big ships use helicopters. Any boat or any ship can turn over out there on the ocean. Huge vessels have turned over. Some of them, they've never heard anything from again.

Not long ago, a storm came through here after dark. Edwin, my son, was bringing a car [automobile] ship out. When he got to the lighthouse, he realized the wind had exceeded what anybody forecasted. He called Bruce, my youngest son, who was bringing out another car ship, and told him, "Don't bring your ship out. The wind's picking up to such a point that it's not safe to come out." But Bruce had already left the dock and couldn't go back. When he got out offshore, the wind was blowing seventy-five to eighty miles an hour. The captain of the ship told Bruce, "You'd better go with me to Charleston. It's not safe to get off here." The pilot boat was already there. But it was one of our new boats, which is more stable because it has two big bumpers about two feet in diameter that run from the bow to the stern. They serve as cushions between the pilot boat and the ship, and they serve as stabilizers. Any pilot has gone out in rough weather, and it can be risky at times. Most of the time, you can get a pretty good lee [protection from the wind] by turning the ship.

Not all of our pilots are fully licensed to take any vessel. We have step-ups as that man improves. Lawrence Gray is pilot number two. Edwin III is pilot number three. I'm still going as pilot one. Bruce is pilot four. Pilot five is John Beieler, from Buffalo, New York. Pilot number six is Jonathan Tennant, from Charleston, South Carolina. We had to change our method of selecting pilots. It's on the point system now. The states that were a part of the original colonies almost all operated on the apprentice system, which means you take a young man and teach him everything about a harbor and piloting it. The Gulf Coast states and West Coast states mostly hired ex-masters. Anything on the apprentice system will produce father-son workers. And I know why it works that way. There were times when I had to go out to a ship at two o'clock in the morning, and I'd hire a boat operator who wouldn't show up. But I knew where my sons were. I'd go and get them and say, "Let's go, boys." Even if they were in school, one of them had to get me on that ship. So you're born into it. Some sons like it, and some don't. The ones who do will follow that trade. But it gets to a point where other people want an opportunity to be pilots, too. Because of that, we've gone to a point system to make our selections. The criteria we use has to be approved by the commandant of the Coast Guard in Washington, D.C. Every five years, our training program has to be reexamined. We hired an ex–Coast Guard man to help set up our system, which the local commission approved.

We have an apprentice now, Jason Kavanaugh, who's in his mid-twenties. His father is a pilot down in Fernandina. Florida works on a different system than Georgia. It's practically impossible for him to become licensed there to work with his dad. In Florida, pilots are accepted by a statewide commission. Whenever a Florida port needs a pilot, they advertise for that port, and they give a test. The one with the highest grade gets the appointment to that port.

NOTES

1. "Ship Hits Georgia Bridge: One Killed and 8 Missing," *New York Times*, November 9, 1972.

2. According to the *Brunswick News* of September 11, 1999, "[Captain, Frank] Stanejko was unhappy with the way the helmsman was responding to the harbor pilot's orders and relieved him of duty shortly before the ship cast off the dock. 'The AB (able seaman) on duty was drunk, so the old man ran him off,' [assistant engineer Henry] Billitz said. 'So they got this other guy, one of these smart aleck AB's who think they know everything. They don't know anything.'"

3. According to the *Brunswick News* of November 14, 1972, "Capt. Frank Stanejko . . . testified that the helmsman steered right when he should have

moved the wheel to the left. Ships leaving a berth in Brunswick must make a tight and complicated left turn to pass through the open span to passage in the Atlantic."

4. *The Islander* of St. Simons Island reported in its November 9, 1972, issue that the cars on the bridge slid off and plunged into the water "like they were coming off an assembly line." The *Brunswick News* of November 8, 1972, told the story of "Mrs. Mary Donal and her new husband, Albert Donal, 36, of Roslyn, Pa. [who] were returning from a 10-day honeymoon in Florida. . . . 'The bridge fell out from under us,' [Mrs. Donal said.] 'I was trapped in the car a couple of minutes. I got out. The window was open on the driver's side. . . . All I heard was a lot of crashing, a lot of screaming.' . . . Their car fell more than 50 feet. . . . She feared her husband had been killed instantly. . . . When she reached the emergency room . . . she found him only a few feet away being treated for a slight concussion and abrasions and bruises. 'He told me he felt I had been one of the victims because I can't swim,' she said." That same issue of the *Brunswick News* included the sad tale of "George Kutchar, a 19-year-old shrimp boat worker [who] was helping look for automobile passengers who had been dumped into the Brunswick River. . . . 'We saw several people floating in the water,' [Kutchar said.] 'I pulled up this woman—her face was down—and when I got her in the boat . . . it was my grandmother.' "

5. The *Brunswick News* of December 7, 1972, carried this headline: "Lanier Bridge Barriers to Go Back Farther: Traffic crossing the Sidney Lanier Bridge, damaged when it was hit by a freighter Nov. 7th will be required to stop a greater distance from the draw span, a state engineer says. . . . 'We certainly recognize that methods of traffic control are available to insure minimum interruption to traffic flow and maximum protection towards future occurrences of this type.' "

Joseph Albert Bruce Faircloth, Jr., and Jane Lou McLeod Faircloth

During World War II, Bruce Faircloth rode to Brunswick on crowded cattle trucks with other Liberty ship workers. Before the war was over, he moved to the area, bringing with him a much-needed commodity for any community—an appreciation of the fine arts.

He recounts life during World War II and his work in helping to establish two local theater groups. Faircloth has served multiple terms as president of the Brunswick Community Concert Association. For many years, he ran his business, B. F. Custom Interiors, on Mallory Street in the village of St. Simons.

At the end of his narrative, his wife, Jane Lou Faircloth, tells an amusing tale about a relative who served in the Civil War.

Bruce: I was born in my parents' house in Douglas, Georgia, at about five-thirty in the morning on December 26, 1925. There were two doctors there, a Dr. Clark and Dr. Cravatt.

The summer of my junior year in high school, I worked at the airport. South Georgia Junior College in Douglas had a landing strip. It was taken over by Raymond-Richardson Aviation Company, who had a contract with the army to teach inductees how to fly an airplane—a Stearman PT-17, a double-cockpit training biplane. A lot of these boys had never been in an airplane before. A number of my classmates and I got summer jobs there in 1940, before World War II. We were called "line boys." There were 115 line boys in groups of five on a concrete apron. Their job was to keep these planes gassed and oiled up and to crank them. You didn't just mash a button and it started. You inserted a crank into the rotor, the magneto part of the engine, until it made a sort of humming sound, like cranking a Model T Ford. You had to put some muscle in it to get it started. While the rotor was still spinning, you took the crank out and yelled, "Contact!" to the pilot, who pulled out the throttle and turned a key, completing an electrical circuit, and it cranked. To turn the rotor, you had to stand on one of the plane's wheels, and the propeller was close by on the front of the fuselage. One day, one of the line boys stumbled while cranking the rotor. They picked his parts up with a shovel.

The pilots kept a log on each plane—how many hours the engine ran, how many gallons of gasoline and quarts of oil were used, and how many hours in the air were logged. At the end of my high-school senior year, my mother and sister moved to Waycross. I stayed in Douglas another year and a half before joining them. I went to South Georgia College during the day and went out to their airport at five o'clock in the afternoon and wrote up the logs in

Joseph Albert Bruce Faircloth, Jr.

another book. They found out I could read and write.

Waycross was where a lot of people from Douglas went to go shopping. It was a railroad town and a sawmill town. It's where north, south, east, west railroads crossed, and the railroads had maintenance shops there. They had a very large dormitory-like structure for their employees at one time. The building may still be standing. We lived in Cherokee Heights, one of the first suburban housing developments in Waycross, about three blocks from the public swimming pool.

This country was cranking up for World War II, and people from all the surrounding counties had gone to Glynn County to work in the shipyard. J. A. Jones Construction Company had the contract to build EC2s, which were Emergency Cargo Carriers—the Liberty ships.[1] They were three masts and three holes. People rode from Kingsland, Woodbine, Waycross, Waynesville, Jesup, Alma—from all the towns around, and the shipyards operated twenty-four hours a day.

My older brother, Shelley Dewey, had gone into the air force and served in England. He first tried to enlist, but they turned him down two or three times because of an ear problem. They finally drafted him into the service.

I was turned down because of a heart murmur, so I got a job at the shipyard and rode to Brunswick on cattle trucks with a bunch of other workers who rode back and forth from Waycross every day. They would pick us up in downtown Waycross and stop along the highway to and from Brunswick. It took about two hours one-way. I would work eight hours and take the two-hour ride back to Waycross. I believe I made $1.20 an hour. We broke for thirty or forty-five minutes for lunch or an evening meal. You either carried your lunch to work with you or ate at one of the shipyard cafeterias. There were five or six buildings scattered throughout the shipyard that served meals cafeteria-style. There was a large cafeteria up near the entrance gate. It was contracted out. Carley Zell was one of the owners of the cafeteria.

I started out as a ship fitter. You had to go to school for about two weeks. I found out that ship fitters mostly swung sledgehammers. I probably weighed 125 pounds and was definitely not sledgehammer-swinging material. I also found out that welders made the most money. Outside shell welders earned the most money because it was dangerous and required first-class welding. There was a shortage of them, always. They worked overtime at time-and-a-half pay. I worked maybe a week out on the yard swinging a sledgehammer and transferred to welding. I went back to a welding school there in the shipyard and passed the welding test in about three days. I went out from the yard and down on the ways, where the final assembly of the ships took place before they were launched. I worked on the scaffolding as an arc welder, which I really enjoyed. I was working there when they launched the first ship they built there [the *James M. Wayne*, launched March 13, 1943]. It was maybe six or eight weeks before the next one was launched. The more we did, the faster and more efficiently we built them. And we ended up doing seven in one month. So the period between launches became shorter and shorter. We built, I believe, about a hundred ships.

The shipyard had an infirmary, which was staffed twenty-four hours a day by a couple of doctors and three or four nurses [see the Gloster Lewis "Buck" Buchanan narrative]. The welders wore leather jackets and leather overalls, and it got pretty hot during the summer months. The back and sides of the overalls were open, so you got some circulation. On the ship's interior, in the holds and inner bottoms, they had electric fans and large ducts that pulled air out and circulated it. In the winter, heaters were used, and the heat was circulated by electric fans.

Brunswick became extraordinarily full of shipyard workers,[2] most of which were real, honest-to-God Georgia crackers. Rooming and boarding houses were absolutely full. I understand, though I never knew anyone who did this, that some of the workers went to the movies and slept there because they couldn't find a bed in Brunswick.

After the war, most of the workers went back to their hometowns. Some, like me, stayed on and worked in the area. After five or six months of shuttling from Waycross to Brunswick, we bought a little cottage, number eight, at Oglethorpe Park on St. Simons, which was one of the first housing developments on the island. My mother, Cordelia, worked as a telephone operator at the Cloister Hotel on Sea Island.

When I came to Brunswick, Windsor Park had just been converted from a golf course into a neighborhood [see the Eleanor Stiles Cate narrative]. There was a tremendous oak tree in the middle of Gloucester Street in Brunswick, about a hundred feet west beyond the intersection with Newcastle. I've forgotten when they took that tree down. It must have been sometime in the early '70s. There was another one in the middle of Gloucester Street near the railroad tracks where Martin Luther King Boulevard is. You had to drive around the trees.

I was also an aircraft spotter during the war. There was an observation tower, made of wood, on St. Simons on Frederica Road in Glynn Haven between where the fire station is now and the marsh. There are three relatively high-elevation spots on St. Simons. One of them is up on the north end. There is one in Glynn Haven, and there is one, incidentally, in Oglethorpe Park right under number eight. There were also observers on the lighthouse and on a tower at the King and Prince Hotel, which was the BOQ [bachelor officers' quarters] for the navy. You had to take training to study aircraft. You studied cards with silhouettes of the outlines of various aircraft. Typically, you manned the observer tower for about four hours at a time during the day. I don't believe it was manned at night.

The naval air station, which was called Glynco, was just north of Brunswick on Highway 17 where the Federal Law Enforcement Training Center is now. There were two very large wooden hangars that housed blimps. At the time, they were the largest wooden structures in the world. The blimps were used to spot German submarines prowling the coast.

There were four, possibly five, merchant ships sunk between Charleston and Jacksonville by subs. On St. Simons, the navy had a school for radar that was sort of secret. Pilots stationed at the airport on St. Simons were trained to cruise up and down the coast and spot U-boats. And they communicated with the base at Glynco so that the blimps could navigate to the site and drop depth charges.

The blimps' ability to hover and move very slowly is what made them important. The reason the navy located the blimp base here was that there were statistically 347 flying days of perfect conditions for blimps to operate. They were not able to operate well in windy, stormy conditions.

You became accustomed on St. Simons to hearing dull thuds, which were the depth charges exploding. You also, particularly on the island, felt a slight tremor through the ground. After a merchant ship was hit, you'd go to the beach and see big blobs of crude oil, diesel fuel, Mae West life jackets, and so on. Occasionally, you'd see splintered timbers, which were part of the cradles that went in the water when Liberty ships were launched. They floated everywhere. This was before the Sidney Lanier Bridge was built, and there was no causeway to Jekyll. So you didn't have to take into account the bridge when launching a ship.

There used to be a lot of eating places with dance floors all over Glynn County. On St. Simons, there was the Trophy Club down in the village. The Cofers had a place that was on pilings over what is now beach at the pier where the old St. Simons Hotel used to be. The King and Prince Hotel had a bar, patio, and a dance floor. The

19th Hole was at the intersection of Demere and Frederica roads. It was owned by Franklin Horne. He also owned the Frederica Yacht Club out by Fort Frederica. It was a nice restaurant and bar on an old barge that sat on the inland waterway.

There was a dance floor at the old Oglethorpe Hotel in Brunswick on Newcastle Street. It was a lovely red-brick American Gothic hotel with what I call "wooden icicles"—much wooden gingerbread railings and cutouts above windows and doors.

Sometime in the late '50s, early '60s, they filmed a movie here called *The View from Pompey's Head*, starring Richard Egan, Dana Wynter, and a young DeForest Kelley [later of *Star Trek* fame]. It was based on a book by Hamilton Basso. Some of the scenes were filmed at the Oglethorpe Hotel. My mother got a tiny part in the film. In one scene, you can see her sitting on the porch of the hotel. Eventually, the hotel became unprofitable to operate. The railroad station in back of the hotel closed as passenger travel shifted to automobiles. It was the glory days of the motels, which made very nice downtown hotels rather obsolete. Traffic shifted to Highway 17 and later the interstate highway.

The navy built a gymnasium for the radar school at the St. Simons airport. There may have been some offices there, too. After the war, a little theater group was organized on St. Simons. A stage was added to the gym, and it was turned into the Island Playhouse, which most people simply called "the Playhouse." The theater group on St. Simons was organized by some members of the original Brunswick Little Theatre group in the early 1950s. I had taken some fine-arts courses at the University of Georgia and got involved with the Brunswick theater company. There were other people in the county who were very interested in the performing arts from all backgrounds. There were schoolteachers and electrical, structural, and chemical engineers who worked at the Hercules Powder Company and at the pulp mill. They were interested members, and we organized the Brunswick Little Theatre.

One of the first plays we did was *Arsenic and Old Lace.* Our first productions were staged in the Memorial Auditorium on the Glynn Academy campus. That auditorium is owned by the public and is under the management of the board of education. It, as well as the high school and several churches, sits on property donated by Urbanus Dart, who was a large landowner in the early 1800s. If the real estate is used for any other purpose other than religious—or in the case of Glynn Academy and the Memorial Auditorium, educational, civic, or cultural purposes—the title of that land reverts to his heirs, who are still living in Brunswick.

Memorial Auditorium is one of the very few theaters that was a model for the staging of the performing arts, in that it had a full basement beneath the stage that could have been utilized for productions. You know, "Up jumped the devil from a puff of smoke!" That sort of thing. It had footlights and a full loft above for lighting, slides, flats, and so on. Unfortunately, the basement was never used for stage machinery. It housed a coal-fired furnace that created steam heat for the building's radiators. When that furnace was replaced by electric heat, the basement was used for dressing rooms. That stage has been redone twice in my lifetime.

There were three sisters who were Brunswick residents at the time—the McGarvey girls, who lived on Dartmouth Street. They were all maiden ladies, and each one had different intellectual and professional interests. Their brother, Cormac, was an architect for quite a few private homes in Brunswick, St. Simons, Sea Island, and throughout the county. I believe he did one or two buildings in Waycross and Jesup. Miss Virginia was most interested in music and had taught it professionally. Her younger sister Margaret was secretary to the superintendent of Hercules Powder Company. She was very interested in drama and the stage. The youngest sister, Mary, dabbled in all the arts. Professionally, she was employed by one of the state agencies in Atlanta as a social worker. When she came home to Brunswick, she was involved in the arts. The McGarvey girls were primary movers and shakers of the Community Concert organization and the [Brunswick] Little Theatre.

The St. Simons theatrical group came about because there was some disagreement among the membership as to the selection of plays to be presented. We were doing productions for family audiences. No four-letter words. No sensational plots. The avant-garde theater at that time was Tennessee Williams. It was the early days of Carson McCullers, *The Member of the Wedding*, etc. The people who wanted to put on those sorts of plays organized the St. Simons Little Theatre about 1954 or 1955. I was a member of both groups. So was my wife, Jane. Our first performances were at the Island Playhouse by the airport—the old navy gym. We didn't begin using the old Casino by the St. Simons Pier until after the movie theater closed sometime in the 1960s. The St. Simons Little Theatre put on many of the Broadway musicals in the '50s and '60s, like *Gypsy, Fiddler on the Roof, Oklahoma*, almost all of the Ethel Merman Broadway shows. We had a couple of gals and a couple of men who had extraordinarily good theatrical voices. One actress, a Norwegian lady who came to Brunswick during the war, went on to New York and got a few roles in some plays. One of the announcers at a local radio station, WMOG, joined the St. Simons group. His name was Bill Groves. He later went on to become a [television] news anchor for many years in Jacksonville.

I've held practically every office there is with the local Community Concert—president, vice president, treasurer, and so on. The Community Concert organization was organized in 1940 or 1941. It was started by two young men who worked for the Columbia Broadcasting System to give employment to serious artists for a longer period of the year. Concert seasons for the big cities were only the fall and winter months. There was no such thing

Bruce Faircloth (with Ann Harris Morrison) in the 1951 Brunswick Little Theatre production of "Goodbye My Fancy."

as a concert season in the spring and summer. That was in the 1920s and '30s, well into the 1940s. These two young men had the idea of putting together a roster of artists who would go on the road and give concerts for about a nine-month period, from September through the end of May. If they could make [identify] small- to medium-sized towns with an auditorium or facility that could be used as a concert hall, they would contract with the local groups to book the artists twelve to eighteen months in advance. It's somewhat comparable to the old Chautauqua circuits [of lectures, concerts, and plays] that ran at the turn of the century. The old opera house in Abbeville, Georgia, was on that circuit.

The first concert that I remember coming to Brunswick was the Metropolitan Opera soprano Helen Jepson. That was about 1941. We had the Joffrey II Ballet here twice. Ronald Reagan's son, Ron, Jr., was a member of the troupe the first time we had them. For some of the dance groups, we had to have a masseuse or a chiropractor to be backstage in case they pulled a ligament or sprained an ankle.

The most memorable performers were a group of children called the Little Angels of South Korea. They had appeared on *The Ed Sullivan Show* sometime in the mid-1960s. It was a group of fifty to sixty children between the ages of eight up to about twelve or fourteen, boys and girls and an accompanying orchestra of eight to ten musicians playing native instruments. I've never seen a group of children as well disciplined and well behaved. We had to seat them in one of the classrooms backstage. Those children were in ecstasy over the fresh fruit, particularly the bananas and oranges. The group stayed at one of the local motels and traveled with three or four hot plates. They prepared the food for those children backstage. Those were probably two of the best-attended performances we ever had. Our auditorium was absolutely filled. People were standing along the side walls and across the back.

The other concert that was so very well attended was the dual pianists Ferrante and Teicher. We had the dual pianists Gold and Tisdale three or four times. We had them when they were in their twenties, when they were just beginning, and we had them when they were in their forties and fifties.

Everybody knows about Misha [Mikhail Baryshnikov] and the White Oak Project.[3] The Gilman brothers, who owned Gilman Paper Mill in St. Marys, Georgia, bought three or four thousand acres and built a lodge, which they used for themselves and their guests. They stocked it with all sorts of exotic animals like giraffes and African antelopes. This was in the 1970s and '80s. One of the brothers was a dance aficionado and became friends with Rudolf Nureyev and later Mikhail Baryshnikov. In the mid-1970s, he built a dance studio near St. Marys and formed a dance foundation, the White Oak Dance Project.

When they put in Interstate 95, it went through property owned by the McCarthys [near St. Marys]. They weren't happy about their property being divided by the highway. The road builders needed sand of a particular kind for the foundation of the highway. The McCarthys agreed to let the government build the interstate across their property on two conditions. One was that they construct a bridge over I-95 so the McCarthys could go from one part of their property to the other. It's perhaps the only bridge on I-95 that is not public. The other stipulation was that the government put a clay lining on the hole of a sandpit they dug so it could be used as a fishpond. Baryshnikov was reared by his grandparents in a small town on the Baltic. They were fishermen and used to take him fishing with them. One of the overseers at White Oak knew some of the McCarthys and knew that Baryshnikov would rather fish than dance. So Baryshnikov used to fish from that pond.

Jane: My grandfather's brother, George Fletcher McLeod, was injured in the Battle of Bull Run and left for dead on the battlefield. Later, after he had been found, they discovered the wound in the back of his head had been infected, but that maggots had cleaned it. They needed something they could sterilize to cover the wound in his skull, so they beat a silver dollar with a hammer to fit the hole and pulled the skin over it.

After he recovered, George McLeod was sent to Savannah to

Jane Lou McLeod Faircloth and Joseph Albert Bruce Faircloth, Jr.

be in charge of the quartermaster corps that was making salt out of seawater, which was one of the most treasured commodities in the South at that time.

When the Civil War ended, he went home to farm in Wilcox County at a place called "the Premises" near Abbeville, Georgia, where he became a county commissioner. He was on the commission when the Wilcox County Courthouse was built, and his name is on the cornerstone.

I guess nobody thought anything about that silver dollar being in the back of his head until he was old and baldheaded, which is when I as a child remember him. We thought it was so funny that we could stand behind him and see this silver dollar in his head. You could *see* the dollar! It was very distinct.

He was a funny old man. He was not too tall and had a long white beard, and he ate with his knife. We always thought that was so amusing. I guess it was easier to use a knife to get through that beard to his mouth. The other thing that I remember about him is that he said if Lincoln had lived, Reconstruction would have been entirely different. He thought Lincoln would have done a much better job with Reconstruction. I think that's interesting because all the time I was studying antebellum history, you didn't find many Confederate veterans who made that statement. He was very good and very kind and very gentle, and not at all what you would have thought a warrior would be.

He owned land that went all the way to the Ocmulgee River. They would cut timber and float it to Darien. They would send men on a raft with it to Darien, and they would walk back to Wilcox County.

When I was in high school, George McLeod's son was cutting timber down there one day and found a tree with his father's initials and the year, sometime in the 1880s. They featured that story one Sunday in a magazine section in the *Atlanta Journal* called "It Happened in Georgia."

NOTES

1. A historical marker at the intersection of Bay Street and Gloucester Avenue in Brunswick reads, "Between 1942 and 1944, a skilled labor force of over 16,000 men and women worked in service to the Allied war effort, producing 99 steel vessels for the U.S. Merchant Marines. These vessels served as both cargo and troop carriers, and their reputation for keeping vital supply lines open earned them the name of 'Liberty Ships.' Each month, dedicated shipyard workers produced four of these 447-foot, 3500-ton steel vessels. During December 1944, with the 'Battle of the Bulge' raging in Europe, the Navy requested six ships. In response, these determined patriots built an astounding seven 'Liberty Ships.' The J. A. Jones Construction Company and the people they employed in Brunswick's shipyards came to symbolize the patriotic duty and tireless efforts of America's wartime home front."

2. Edwin H. Ginn, *The First Hundred Years: A History of the American National Bank of Brunswick* (Brunswick, Ga.: Glover Printing Company, 1989), 66. Ginn notes that "the population of Brunswick jumped from 15,000 to 60,000. Housing had to be built for this influx of people, and schools for their children."

3. http://www.findarticles.com/p/articles/mi_m1083/is_n3_v68ai_14884412, accessed February 5, 2007. The article states, "These days [1994] Baryshnikov's quiet passion is the White Oak Dance Project. . . . The troupe embodies the work and ideals of a small, elite body of dancers and choreographers devoted to commissioning and performing new and contemporary works. . . . The genesis of the group goes back . . . to 1975 . . . when Baryshnikov, recuperating from a badly sprained ankle, was . . . a guest of wealthy businessman and philanthropist Howard Gilman, whose company owns the seven-thousand-acre White Oak Plantation on the Florida-Georgia border. The estate comprises a wildlife preserve . . . in addition to a well-equipped gymnasium and dance studio."

Jonathan Lorenzo Williams

Born in the settlement of Hog Hammock on Sapelo Island, Jonathan Williams is a true American success story. His mother worked at the "big house" for R. J. Reynolds, Jr., the tobacco fortune heir. Upon moving to St. Simons, Williams became good friends with another island child, Jim Brown, destined for the NFL Hall of Fame and a string of Hollywood movies. Williams spent much of his childhood on both islands and still has a home on Sapelo.

After earning a college degree and serving in the army, he helped pave the way for racial equality as the head football coach of a predominantly white high school in the early days of integration. Williams has served several terms as a city commissioner in Brunswick—a long way from growing up on a remote barrier island during the Great Depression.

I was born on January 29, 1934, in a section of Sapelo Island, Georgia, called Hog Hammock.[1] My family goes back to the slave days of Sapelo. My parents were Samuel and Ophelia Williams. The lady who delivered me, Katie Underwood, was the midwife over there. She delivered the children on the island. The newest [Sapelo-Meridian] ferry, the *Katie Underwood,* is named after her.

My mom worked in the big house on Sapelo for the R. J. Reynolds [Jr.] family until that was phased out. Then we moved to St. Simons in order to find jobs. My father worked for Sea Island [Company] with Mr. Baumgardner, in landscaping. My mother did maid work several places.

I was between two places—Sapelo and St. Simons. My grandmother reared me on Sapelo. We grew our vegetables and many of the staples we had. Most of the things we ate came out of the fields. As a young boy, I fished and hunted. Life was good. The life I lived I thought was very good.

We had no electricity at all on Sapelo, not in the black area. We had lamplight. When night came, it was dark. Many of the houses didn't have glass windows. They had board shutters. You just closed them up.

You didn't get too hot or too cold. We endured the weather. There wasn't any such thing as air conditioning. We didn't have mosquito control like you have today, but for some reason it didn't seem as bad as it is now. I don't know what the difference is. Mosquitoes and sand flies—those things came and left. You knew when they were coming and prepared for them as best you could, and then they disappeared. During the winter, there was always a fire going in the fireplace. You came in and got warm.

For fun on Sapelo, we'd get together on Saturdays and played baseball and softball. Sunday was all church. On Monday, it was

Jonathan Lorenzo Williams

back to school. I went to school in a one-room schoolhouse on Sapelo, which was located next to St. Luke's Church [founded in 1884]. It is now the church annex. My first teachers were Nellie Gilbert, from Darien, and Miss Susie Wilson, who was an islander, as far as I know. There may have been twenty or thirty children in that school. It went to the sixth grade. Everybody was in one room, and one teacher taught everything.

The teacher would handle us first and move up through the other grades. When the teacher finished with you, you sat down and were quiet. You listened to what she was telling the upperclassmen. I'd sit there listening to her teaching a grade or two ahead of me. When I got to the second grade, I knew a whole lot of what was going on, and I progressed that way. You had to pay attention, and if you were smart enough, you learned a whole lot of things that were being taught to the third- or fourth-graders. It's amazing how it worked so well, compared to what we have now. We had students who left out of that setting and went to other schools and moved up a grade because they knew the work. The teacher had to be a genius to teach all the different grades and control all the age levels in that one room.

After school, you came back home and had chores to do around the house. Most people had chickens, hogs, milk cows. There was always a horse. Everybody had some means of transportation, like a wagon and something to pull it—a horse or an ox.

Sunday was dedicated to church. That's what you did. There was no playing on Sunday. You had church three times a day—very early in the morning, midday, and you'd go back around six o'clock in the evening. The deacons and preacher and their wives sat in a special section. Kids weren't allowed to sit in the back because they probably thought we'd be distracting. An usher would come and really hammer you. Someone was always looking at you. If one of the elders just looked at you, you knew to stop.

The church I went to was called the First AB [African Baptist] in the [Raccoon] bluff area. St. Luke was in the Hog Hammock area on the southern end of the island. On the first Sunday, it was our annual treat to go from Hog Hammock to the bluff, about two and a half miles. Either you walked or rode in a horse-drawn wagon. One person had a flatbed truck, and you put in your reservation a month ahead. But most people had wagons or walked.

They used to baptize right behind where St. Luke is now, on what was called "the baptism ground." There was a creek that ran up in there. That's where they held baptisms.

Once in a while, you left the island to Meridian or Darien or maybe even Brunswick or Savannah. To get to the mainland, you had to take a boat. As a young man, I knew you couldn't ride the boat every day. There were certain days when blacks were privileged to ride the boat. Some days, you weren't permitted. It used to be a thirty-minute ride from Sapelo to Meridian, but the newer boats cut that time in half. When the weather is bad, the Coast Guard will notify the captains that they think it's too rough for the boats to run.

When a hurricane came through, they told everybody to leave Hog Hammock and go down to the south end of the island. That's where, I imagine, the buildings were capable of protecting you from the storm. As a kid, I don't remember that many hurricanes coming through. That was the procedure at that time. Now, if there is a threatening storm, they evacuate the island. There are some diehards who ride it out. Sapelo is kind of lucky, even though it juts out into the ocean. For some reason, the good Lord steers storms around it.

I go back to Sapelo every chance I get. I'm active in SICARS [the Sapelo Island Cultural and Revitalization Society]. We have a big cultural festival where some of the old ways of living are displayed. It's a chance for people to see what the island is like.

Sapelo is a grand place, a beautiful island. It's one of the places on the East Coast that is almost like the good Lord made it. There hasn't been a lot of change over there. Even with the coming of electricity and vehicles, the island hasn't changed that much. You can still see evidences of what it used to be.

There were people there who were either a part of freedom—when the slaves were freed—or close to it, who were old enough to tell us about those things. They go way back. They may or may not have been slaves themselves, but their parents were slaves. Mr. Allen Green was one of the older people over there. He was an interesting man. He could tell you a whole lot of stories about the island. My only regret is that I didn't talk to him on tape. He told me that he would permit me to do that, but I never got around to doing it. The next thing I knew, he slipped away from us.

During World War II, a merchant ship got torpedoed off of St. Simons. That morning, you could hear something rumbling in the background. The news was that a ship had been torpedoed.

The blimps were [moored] at Glynco. You could see the [two] hangars from a long distance away. They were the largest wood structures in America at that time.

The naval officers lived at what is the King and Prince Hotel now. King's Terrace and other places on the island were established as housing during that time.

The Coast Guard had beach patrols on the Sapelo beaches. They rode horses. These well-groomed horses used to come through the Hog Hammock area. They had Jeeps, too.

I was around twelve years old when we left Sapelo, right after World War II, and moved to St. Simons Island. We lived on Harlem Lane, on the south end of the island. Harlem Lane is now called George Lotson Lane. There were a bunch of rental houses owned by J. C. Strother. Harlem ran into Proctor Lane, which is now called Mallory Street, and circles on to Johnson Lane and runs on to

Emmanuel Baptist Church on Demere Road.

They changed the name of Proctor Lane to Mallory Street, which I think is a mistake. The Proctors were leading citizens there. There were three or four brothers who were businessmen. Willis Proctor's convenience store was on the corner of Proctor Lane and Demere Road. There used to be a log cabin on Proctor Lane. An Indian who everyone called "Redman" lived there. There was an old man, Mr. Green, who lived on our street. He owned a taxi business. We called him "Dad."

When I came to St. Simons Island, I went to a two-room school called South End. My teacher on St. Simons was Mr. Ralph Baisden, who was from either Brunswick or McIntosh County. I got special permission to leave the school on St. Simons to go to school in Brunswick. Normally, you would not leave until you reached the seventh grade. But you could get special permission if you wanted to and if you furnished your own transportation. There were not school buses for blacks at that time. The bus we rode was a regular city bus. It cost maybe a quarter a day. If I remember correctly, the board of education paid the twenty-five-cent fee if you were in the eighth or ninth grade. But if you were in the seventh grade, you were there a year before you were scheduled to go to Brunswick, so you had to pay your way. That's what I did. I believe the bus company name was called Tidewater. It ran from Brunswick to St. Simons and Sea Island. It was the main transportation for black citizens if you didn't have a car.

I went to Risley High in Brunswick, which was a pretty famous school at the time, from 1949 to 1953. We had great teachers and a great principal, Mr. J. S. Wilkerson. Risley was recognized all over Georgia.[2] Many of the graduates went to college out of state. I went to Bethune-Cookman College, down in Daytona Beach. The graduating class I was a part of was extraordinary because of the number of people who went on to higher learning, which was probably 60 percent or more, and held good positions and did well afterward. I'm not saying there weren't other good classes at Risley, but this was the one I was a part of. Risley has always been recognized. Risley was one of the few schools that had twelve grades, which put us ahead of some of the students from other places. Most of the other schools had only eleven grades. You graduated after the eleventh grade. Whereas students from other schools might have trouble getting into a college, Risley students really didn't have those problems. Our grade averages were really good, something like ninety-five to a hundred. Most of the colleges knew about Risley's graduates, and they recruited us. A lot of people may not understand what I'm saying.

I don't know of one black teacher who lost a position after desegregation here in Brunswick. Most of the teachers at Risley went to Glynn Academy or Brunswick High. After Risley High was closed, it became a sixth-grade center. The principal at Risley at that time, Walter C. McNeely, became its principal. His wife taught music. She made me get in the school choir. Plus, we had the Hi Y Club, which is similar to the FCA—Federation of Christian Athletes—today. It fostered the religious part of education.

I went to Emmanuel Baptist Church on St. Simons. For baptisms, you dressed in a white gown and walked from the church down Demere Road to the beach—all the way down to the pier section. They had a special area where we had baptisms. The tide would be going out, and the minister would establish the place for the baptism, and you were "drowned" in the ocean. They buried me in the ocean. There was no part of you showing when they dunked you under the water. They got all of the sin out of you. They washed it away from you. After that, I walked all the way back home and changed clothing. It was winter when I got baptized. It was cold, but I was twelve years old, and I could take anything. The man who baptized me was Reverend Chandler. He was replaced by Reverend

Leggett, who has been at the church for the last fifty-two years.

Jim Brown and I grew up together on St. Simons. He and I were playmates. You could see his athleticism then. Jim, myself, and Andrew Phillips played together. For some reason, no one challenged us. We weren't bullies, but we might have been more physical than a lot of the other boys we dealt with. He has a daughter on St. Simons who lives in the house he grew up in.[3]

When Jim was in his glory days, he came back to the island several times. When I was coaching at Brunswick High, I once told my players that I grew up with Jim Brown. They didn't believe it. Then one day, one of them told me, "I saw Jim Brown last night." I said, "No, you didn't. No such thing." He said, "Yes, I did, coach. He's staying at Sea Palms."

So I called the motel and asked if Jim Brown was registered there. They said, "Yes, he is registered here." I asked, "Is he taking calls?" They said, "Well, he didn't say he wasn't taking calls. I'll ring him for you." Sure enough, he rang the room, and Jim answered the phone. And I was a little reluctant. I thought, *Hey, this guy's forgotten all about me.* So I said, "Hey, Jim. This is B. J." For some reason, I got the nickname "B. J." growing up. Don't ask me what it stands for because I don't know. Anyway, he was elated. Man, you could hear him hollering, "Hey, my man!" So we had a good conversation. I told him I was coaching at Brunswick High and that I would like for him to come and talk to my team. He didn't hesitate. He said, "I'll be over there tomorrow."

Sure enough, he came over to Brunswick, and he looked like the Hulk coming across the field. And boy, my kids were just amazed. Jim told them that he grew up on the island and what happened to him when he left, some of the challenges. I think at that time he had just retired from football and went into the movies. Some of the kids asked him why he quit football. I believe at that time he had just done *The Dirty Dozen* movie. He said, "Well, I just wanted to do something else. The challenge I had was someone told me I couldn't be an actor, so I wanted to prove that I can be an actor."

Believe it or not, we had fun growing up on the island. We would have roller-skate races from the East Beach Causeway bridge to Demere Road, and we'd skate all the way to Fort Frederica and back. The roller-skate wheels were made of steel, and you carried spares in your pocket. So when you wore out a wheel, you stopped, put another one on, and kept going.

It was my junior or senior year when they built a little ball field, Demere Park, for us to play on. We had games there on the weekends. We also had Scout meetings. One of the things we did after a Scout meeting was to go out and play football.

As far as race relations go during that time, it was kind of an established thing. We knew where we could go, and we went there. No one actually bothered us. Sometimes, for instance, when we were walking home, the white school bus would pass us, and the kids would spit out the window and call us the "N" word. But we didn't go around fighting anybody.

All of us had something to do. We weren't idle like some kids are today. We had jobs after school. Saturday mornings were very busy. By daylight, I'd be out raking or mowing a yard, or head to the Sea Island Golf Course to be a caddy. Most of the people I caddied for were guests of Sea Island. The first person I caddied for was a sailor from the base on St. Simons. In the evening, I'd come home and do something around the house.

I used to fish using what we called a hand line, which was nothing more than a cord with a hook and a sinker. But you caught just as many fish as anybody else with expensive reels. You threw it out, and it would settle down. By the time it settled, a fish would hit it, and you reel it in with your hands. Or you'd use a bamboo pole.

We fished on East Beach at Gould's Inlet. At one time, you could drive on the beach almost down to the last house. Hurricane

Dora came and took all the beach away from there. That's one of the areas, on the very north end of East Beach, where we could go swimming. The other place we used to go swimming was near the Sea Island Golf Course. After a day of caddying, we walked across what was the practice area of the golf course to the beach there. But besides the pier, those were about the only places you [African-Americans] could go at that time. For movies, we'd go to the Roxy on the corner of H and Albany streets in Brunswick. It was the black movie theater. The building is still there.

I used to be a paperboy for the *Brunswick News*, along with Andrew Phillips. We rode bikes. I used to throw papers all around the King and Prince area, all the way down to East Beach, and the entire South End black area. The newspapers were shipped over from Brunswick on a bus and dropped off on the corner of Arnold Road and Ocean Boulevard, right there where The Still is. If we had something afterwards we wanted to do, it would take maybe an hour and a half to do the route. After we delivered our papers, we'd ride on the beach back from East Beach to the King and Prince. I would say there were a hundred-plus people on the route. The Baumgardners, Gilberts, and the Goulds were on my route.

One of the black no-nos growing up was you did not wear your hat in a building. Now, I see people sitting down eating with their hats on. During my day, you just didn't do that. When I go into a building, my hat comes off of my head. I wouldn't dare put a hat on my head while I'm eating.

Going north on Demere Road past the airport, there was a little settlement there around Longview [see the Neptune Small and Diane Cassandra Palmer Haywood narrative]. Then you didn't see anything else until you got to Glynn Haven. And from Glynn Haven, you didn't see anything else until you got to Harrington. The Red Barn was one of the first things built there. I would hunt in the woods between those areas. It was just forest back then. We'd hunt squirrels, rabbit, raccoons, whatever was there. Sea Palms was a hunting area.

We used to fish a lot of places, especially Dunbar Creek. That's where Ebo's Landing is. You knew about what happened at Ebo's Landing, but it wasn't so sacred that you couldn't catch a fish out of there. Now, it's private property.

Arnold Road, on the south end of St. Simons, used to be heavy with clubs when it was a shell road. On the corner of Arnold and Demere roads lived a lady named Hattie Follins. Right there almost in her front yard was a restaurant called Bobby Dock Chicken Shack. On the other corner, across from where Jim Brown lived, was a nightclub. Down from him, Willis Proctor's brother had a fruit stand and fish market where I used to work. Further down Arnold Road, almost across from Edwin Fendig's business, was a nightclub run by a Proctor. Right next to Fendig's was Sam Proctor's home. Near Proctor Lane, on Demere Road where the convenience store is now, there used to be a famous club called the LaQuartz Club. Jasper Barnes and his brother were the owners. Neptune Small was Jasper's great-granddaddy or something like that. Next to it, where they are now putting up condos, was a club called the Blue Inn. That was the first club I was allowed to go in. Doc Sausage, a homeboy who went and made it big, was playing there. He came up with a hit song called "Rag Mop." He was from this area.[4]

The only hurricane I really remember was Dora. Dora changed things. It changed the pier section and a whole lot of East Beach. President [Lyndon B.] Johnson came through the area. I saw him. He came from the island and went somewhere down on the south end of Brunswick. Then he came back up Albany [Street], turned the corner, and went downtown. I saw him on the corner of Albany and Gloucester. He paused there and shook hands with a lot of people. One lady who shook his hand ran away and screamed, "I'm not ever going to wash my hand." I didn't shake his hand, but I was there.

When I was in college, I wanted to be a coach, so I majored in health and physical education. When I graduated, I got drafted. I had my diploma in one hand and my draft papers in the other. So I did my time in the service, and I enjoyed it. Back then, everybody got drafted. I didn't mind at all. I sort of looked forward to going into the service. In fact, if I didn't get a scholarship to go to college, I would have made a career in the military.

I was in special services. My battalion was stationed in Nuremberg, Germany. I loved Germany. It's a different kind of cold, but it didn't bother me. Their forests are like our national parks. It's clean. The German people do a lot of walking. In my spare time, I'd get a bicycle and ride through the villages.

The thing that got me to Germany was football. I played in Berlin and most of the major cities in Germany, which afforded me the chance to see a lot of the country. The army had several teams over there. There were three All-American football players on my team.

During the time that I was getting ready to leave the army, I sent out letters indicating that I was looking for a coaching job. I sent one to Coffee County, and the principal there had contacted my coach at Risley, L. J. Lomax,[5] to see if he would leave Brunswick and go to Douglas, Georgia. So Lomax recommended me, and I got a letter from the principal in Douglas. I got out of the army just in time to start coaching there. A good friend of mine, Lambert Reed, and I were almost co–head coaches there because he was a local homeboy and an All-American at Morris Brown College in Atlanta. We worked together. Whoever was handy at the time acted as head coach.

We did that for a year before he moved to Miami. So I was head coach there for three more years. Then Coach Lomax got a job at Fort Valley State as the head coach there. He recommended me to come to Brunswick to be the head coach at Risley High. I had a pretty good record at Risley. After integration, I went to Brunswick High as the head coach in 1969. Brunswick High, up to that point, hadn't been established too long as a football team and hadn't won a game. I was head coach there for ten years.

When I got into coaching in 1959, you knew you were going, and you knew what you had to go up against. We knew where we were. We were all black. That's what we were. There wasn't the idea of trying to integrate a football team back then. During 1969 and 1970—when mass integration came—is when things really changed. I had the same success coaching a mixed team as I did when I had an all-black team. I didn't have the problem a lot of other places had because I was appointed the head coach at a predominantly white school. When I went to my first meeting with those kids, they were enthusiastic about me coming. There was some opposition all right—not a whole lot—and I'm sure there were some kids who didn't play because their parents didn't want them playing for me. But the kids came out, and I didn't see anyone boycotting because I was a black man. They came out and played.

I had a booster club that did the things they had to do to make sure the team was good. The football was a big part of integration at Brunswick High, and there were some black students who were on the team the year before integration. If it wasn't for the football team and the way they got along, there were a whole lot of other things that would not have gone true at Brunswick High. Our football team took a positive lead in trying to make sure that school stayed open.

But there was not a whole lot of college recruiting of black athletes in those days. I once went to a clinic in Atlanta in the early '70s, and the question was asked of someone when would he recruit black players. He said, "I would recruit them tomorrow, but my alumni association is not going to let me play them. There's no sense in me trying to go against my alumni association. They're the ones paying the bills."

Those were the days when Alabama would go to play in a bowl game on the West Coast and got killed. And they got killed by teams with black players on them. Bear Bryant said that as soon as the alumni association permitted him to sign black players, he was going to get them, because he was not going to go back to one of these bowls games and get killed by black players.

Coaching was my life. I wish I could stay forever young and be a coach. Sometimes, the kids I had come back to town and look me up. Some of them have really made good. One player, one of my captains, Ronald Mells, is a professor at one of the big Midwestern schools. Carnell Seymour was recruited by Georgia Tech on an academic scholarship and worked in Saudi Arabia with an oil company. John Brown is a big realtor in Atlanta. Those are just a few. I've got kids all over the country now in good positions. They do not hesitate to come back to me and say, "Hey, coach, I really appreciate what you did for me."

I was really interested in their grades. I talked to their teachers, who would notify me if they were slipping. The main thing is that I had respect for my kids and from my kids. I didn't have many of the problems coaches have today. I did have a few that I had to go to their home and get them out of bed and bring them to school. I had some boys who were thinking about quitting school. I'd go and bring them to school. I'd say, "You've got to go!" Most of the time, these things happen after the football season is over. Some people might think I was just interested during the football season. No. I was interested the year round, and they knew that.

But coaching has changed the same way teaching has changed. We just don't have the privilege of doing the things to make sure that our players realize the sacrifice they have to make in order to win. In other words, it's just like in the classrooms. You cannot do the things that you used to do. You cannot raise your voice at a player to let him know that, "Hey, this is what has to be done if we're going to win." And you'd better not put your hand on him. These are the things that have changed since I was a coach. When I was coaching, the kids knew that they had to do what I asked them to do, or there were little penalties they had to pay if they were going to be part of the team. All of them accepted what they had to do. Coaching is different. Kids are different. Football used to be just about the only game in town. Now, a lot of kids would rather run around in their cars than running and sweating on a football field. We still have boys out there who really want to play and will pay the price in order to play and win. But there are some places where those kinds of traditions aren't there anymore. In the Golden Isles, there are so many other distractions and other things that kids can do.

My wife, Lolan, and I were married for forty-five years as of last August 17. We've both given each other the best years of our lives. So now that she's sort of incapacitated, it's incumbent on me that I do the very best I can to help her, to make sure she's taken care of. We got married because we were in love. She grew up in Clayton, Alabama, which is nineteen miles past Eufaula, going towards Montgomery. Her maiden name was Person. We met while we were both in Douglas, Georgia, as teachers.

The reason we didn't move back to St. Simons was because there were ten of us children in my parents' house. The house was really crowded. So there was no need for me to try to move back to St. Simons. I was closer to my job, and the opportunity came for me to own my own home, so I built a house here in Brunswick.

I had no desire to be a city commissioner. But there were some people who talked to me who said, "There's a chance that you can possibly be a city commissioner. We think that you can do a good job. Would you consider the idea of running?" I told them I really didn't want to do that. I'm not political in any kind of way. But I was encouraged by so many people that I put my hat in the ring, and I won. Actually, Ken Plyman was in the middle of his term, and he decided to run for mayor. So that position was left open. I got in for the two years remaining on his term, then I had to run again against seven people and got elected again. I've got two more years on my present four-year term.

I enjoy serving the people. I've always been a people person. Anytime I can help somebody, I try to do that. I think this is what being a city commissioner is all about. You try to make things better for everybody. I tell people that I'm a city commissioner for everybody. I love Brunswick. It's my home. I'd like to see this city grow and be one of the leading cities on the Eastern Seaboard. You're not appreciated a lot of times. People get mad with you and forget everything that you've ever done that is good. But that's part of the job. If you got in the business for people to like you, then you need to get out.

NOTES

1. William S. McFeely, *Sapelo's People: A Long Walk into Freedom* (New York and London: W. W. Norton & Company, 1994), 14, 83. The author writes, "Sapelo's people today are descendants of slaves of Thomas Spalding, who died in 1851." He explains that the name Hog Hammock comes from former slave Sampson Hogg, whose "family changed its name to Hall long after the [Civil] war."

2. Benjamin Allen, *Glynn County, Georgia: Black America Series* (Charleston, S.C.: Arcadia Publishing, 2003), 46. The author writes, "The original Risley Grammar School was located on Albany Street at the corner of 'I' Street. It was named after Douglas Gilbert Risley (1838–1882) who arrived in Glynn County in 1866 with the Bureau of Refugees, Freedman, and Abandoned Lands."

3. Ibid., 78. Allen notes that "James Nathaniel Brown was born in 1936 on St. Simons Island and was raised by his grandmother."

4. www.hoyhoy.com/doc.htm, accessed October 10, 2006. The Web site

notes, "Doc Sausage (Lucius Tyson) was the lead singer and drummer in the Five Pork Chops, a frenetic jive group that recorded in the 1940s. . . . In 1950 he recorded with a band called 'Doc Sausage and His Mad Lads' for the Regal label, and these records included 'Sausage Rock' as well as 'Rag Mop' and others."

5. Allen, *Glynn County Georgia*, 54. The author notes that "Leon Lomax graduated with a B.S. from Fort Valley State College in Fort Valley, Georgia and an M.S. from Boston University in Boston, Massachusetts. He was the coach of the [Risley High] 1950 All-Conference Championship team with Edward Lowe, Jonathan Williams, B. J. Phillips, Milton Byard, and Snooks 'Choo Choo' Jones."

George Wallace Baker

A longtime blackwater rescue diver and commercial diver and self-styled "expert on hearsay history on the coast," George Baker brings a unique perspective to area events. He has an intimate knowledge of the Golden Isles from both the air and the underbelly— the area's ocean, rivers, tidal creeks, and sloughs. One of his first search-and-rescue experiences occurred when the African Neptune *hit the Sidney Lanier Bridge in 1972 (see the Edwin Rubel Fendig, Jr., narrative).*

Named for a man (George Wallace) who saved his father's life, Baker has logged hundreds of hours in alligator- and shark-infested waters searching for people and finding objects others don't want found—hijacked cars, guns used in crimes, stolen safes. In an interview with the Brunswick News, *he called Georgia's coast " 'the last treasure coast,' a largely unexplored stretch where muddy water and an abundance of sharks have deterred scavengers from being able to prove the tales of lost gold and precious jewels."[1]*

I was born in Miami, Florida, on August 15, 1947. My daddy, Miles Baker, was with the CAA [Civilian Aviation Administration], which is now the FAA [Federal Aviation Administration]. We lived on the Panhandle of Florida, in Cross City. We're half Seminole Indian on his side of the family.

My mother, Julia Baker, was Black Irish. She was born the night the *Titanic* sunk. My pop transferred to Brunswick when a post became open. He was a reserve deputy, as I am now here, and he became an auxiliary policeman in Brunswick, which is what got me into the rescue line of work. By then, he and my mother, Julia Baker, had divorced. He and my stepmother, Juanita, and I moved to Glynn County when I was ten.

Pop was a story in himself—arctic explorer, Coast Guard rescue guy from World War II. He was fifteen when he lied his way into the Coast Guard. By then, he had already been a deck hand on a tugboat and learned to fly an airplane. When he wasn't working at the FAA, he was [tobacco heir] R. J. Reynolds [Jr.'s] pilot and bodyguard for years. They had a couple of de Havilland Doves and another plane. The first place I came to in Georgia was Sapelo Island, where Mr. Reynolds had his estate. Pop flew me and my sister, Joni, to Sapelo. There's a four-thousand-foot grass airstrip on the island that was better kept back then than it is now. It was very well maintained, with its own drainage system. The first thing we did was to go over to the Reynolds Plantation and have lunch with the old man, who at that time was probably only in his early fifties. He was quite a guy. Another world explorer and veteran who did his bit for his country.

George Wallace Baker

Back then, we'd fly down to Cumberland Island and camp on the beach and fish.

I went to Glynn County Junior High and later to Glynn Academy High School. I graduated in 1966. Growing up, I spent most of my free time at the airport handling cargo and gassing up planes. I worked at both McKinnon Airport on St. Simons and the Brunswick Air Park, which at that time was on part of what is now the local college campus. It was a four-thousand-foot airport with two paved runways. I'd get out of school and hitchhike over to Fourth Street and help Sam Baker, no relation, close up that airport in the evenings. We'd close that up about seven o'clock at night, and he'd fly me over to McKinnon on St. Simons, and we'd close up there. You can't imagine the amount of air traffic that was at McKinnon Airport in those days. Delta and Eastern airlines ran out of there. There were a couple of smaller airlines and a helicopter operation. There were fifty or more airplanes on that ramp on weekends.

Our first house on St. Simons was in King's Terrace behind the Presbyterian church. When Daddy got on with Mr. Reynolds, we got a bigger house over by the ballpark. Diving has been in my family's blood. My grandfather on my father's side was a hard-hat diver in the Miami River. He wore a big, heavy suit with the brass helmet with an air supply line to the surface. Those were the old days of diving. Daddy was a crash-boat diver in World War II. I did a little bit of everything growing up, but all came back to boats, airplanes, and water.

I got into rescue scuba diving following around my dad, who was an auxiliary policeman. He'd go help the old volunteer rescue squad, which is still the emergency management squad we have today, and we still report to the Glynn County police, although we serve a much larger area in the surrounding counties now.

You never forget your first rescue. It was '67, July, on the south beach at Jekyll. A kid had drowned. We all went out as a team, just kind of splashed and waded and dove until we found him. A little black kid.

The divers and the police have resolved dozens of cases over a long period of time. We have helped resolve cases eight or fifteen years old. Sometimes, they are freak accidents—people driving off the road or over a bridge into the water. Not long ago, a lady went off a bridge in an accident. Had there not been witnesses, you wouldn't know they were missing for a while. Sometimes, the bad guys kidnap people, kill them, take their jewelry, and put the bodies in a trunk.

Normally, in blackwater dives, you just feel your way around things. But we've got some neat gadgets now, side-scan sonars that make an exact picture of what's down there for a couple hundred feet around. We've already used them as far away as Lake Oconee to help find drowning victims. Our rescue chief, Jimmy Durrance, is a real whiz at it. The idea is to swoop into an area and get it over with, so the family doesn't stand around and suffer.

I'm working on a bunch of old missing persons cases. Using our side-scans, we found a boat ramp last fall where the bad guys have been ditching automobiles for a long while. We've got six or seven cars down there and were able to rein in a few at a time because we have to work around currents and tides. But one of them, way out in the middle of the river, is a large sedan, which is the type of car driven by two elderly people—the Roamers, Charles and Katherine—who have been missing for twenty-six years. They were extremely well-respected people from Scarsdale, New York. They were coming back from Miami Easter weekend of April 1980, after a month's vacation, and had checked into the Holiday Inn at Highway 341 and I-95. It was typical of them to check into a motel and then find a nice restaurant. So they apparently left to go to dinner. However, during the 1980s, there had been a number of cases where bad guys would pick out some well-to-do tourists down in Florida and follow them to Georgia and rip off their car or motel room for their jewelry. Now, the last thing the average jewel thief wants is a confrontation. But something went wrong that night. It could be Mr. Roamer drove off one of these old boat ramps, thinking it was a side road, considering it was raining that evening. I've been searching for their car since then. And it's intriguing that a boat ramp we've been searching lately is only four miles from that Holiday Inn on the south side of Glynn County. One day, we'll give them a decent burial. We who stand and wait serve best. We're not rocket scientists, but we're patient.

Most of the time, we just get the VIN [Vehicle Identification Number] and the tag number and give it to the police. My partner, Howard "Hollywood" Henderson, and Buddy Webb and Jimmy Durrance, our chief, have retrieved two or three vehicles out of the water in the last two weeks. Most of them are just accidents where people backed off of a ramp.

We find bodies in the automobiles all the time, if they're recent accidents. That's why we're called in, to get the victims back for the families' sake. You just say a little prayer. "Lord, I'm your instrument to send these people home to their families and give them some closure." Sometimes, you get them back alive. That's when they've got out of the car or out of the boat up on the marsh or floating in the water, and you find them. Sometimes, they get disoriented and wander off into the woods.

I've been doing this thirty-eight years in July 2006, and I've found maybe eight or ten people alive—over a hundred dead. I try not to think about it. We play it down for the families' sake. I'd rather not see it in the paper. The press here, Terry Dixon at the *Florida Times-Union* and Bobby Haven at the *Brunswick News*, are really stand-up people.

We do tracking as well and use cadaver dogs. Hollywood and Buddy can track a snowflake across a parking lot. Recently, we had a child homicide in Wayne County and helped find the child in the woods. The GBI [Georgia Bureau of Investigation] called us because they thought he might be in the water. We found the young one in the woods. He had been killed by his mama.

Most of the rural areas around here can't afford to fund dive teams, so we serve a wide area. Believe it or not, the Okefenokee Swamp is a lot easier to work in than the coastal marshes. There are three main river basins here. The alligators around the Altamaha Basin make the ones in the Okefenokee look like pups. If you see a lot of gators, then there aren't many water moccasins to deal with, so you're not so worried about getting snakebit.

The southeast Georgia coast is the second-largest shark breeding ground in the world. Most of the time, the big sharks are just a nuisance. But when you see one, you don't want to make the old boy mad. Sometimes, you have to bump one in the head with a hammer, bearing in mind that whether it's a shark or an alligator, you're trespassing. You're there to snatch back something you want.

I've done a lot of commercial diving. That's how you make money to pay for your rescue gear. I've worked on nine or ten bridges, including the Sidney Lanier Bridge across the Brunswick River. Divers do the templates, set the pilings, jack-ups, and other construction you wouldn't normally associate with diving.

When the old Sidney Lanier Bridge was struck by the *African Neptune*, there was a great loss of life, and a number of cars fell into the water. Some of the victims escaped out of the vehicles but were caught in the current and drowned. The correct orders were given by the pilots, and it was clearly the helmsman's fault. He turned the wheel the wrong way, and when you do that on a big boat, the accident has already happened.

I remember I was at home on St. Simons that night when the phone rang. It was my father calling from the airport. He said, "We're getting reports from pilots that something's happened at the Sidney Lanier Bridge." I couldn't get to the bridge on Highway 17.

So I went down 303 and went up the other way. The boat was still laying alee across the fender system, and the tide was going out. I wasn't really much of a diver back then compared to what I do now, but there wasn't much diving to do that night. There was a northeaster, and the current was terrific. We did go out and get the bodies that were floating and swam them ashore. What I mostly did in that effort was walk out in the marsh and snag bodies. One of the tractor-trailers had dumped a load of fruit crates in the water. Everywhere you looked, your spotlight shined on what you thought could be a human.

It took about three days to sort out who went in the water and who survived and probably a week to determine who was there and who wasn't. You'd hear stories, like a hysterical Greyhound bus dispatcher calling and saying, "I heard about the bridge disaster and can't find a tour bus!" We had so many conflicting reports. I remember one was a truckdriver. He got out of the rig, and his buddy didn't.

I was very active then in the auxiliary police and was out and about with the detectives. I found a striker on a shrimp boat who said he wanted to talk to them. He was living on Jekyll Island at the time, and his girlfriend was allegedly seeing someone else, so he went over to Brunswick the night of the bridge accident to confront her. Well, he gets stuck in traffic on the south end of the bridge waiting for the *African Neptune* to pass through. He hears the ship blowing the danger signal, and he knows what's going to happen when that boat smacks the bridge. It's going to come down. So he runs out on the bridge beating on people's windows, screaming, "Get out of the car and run!" And some of them did. But all the others saw was this wild-haired hippy shrimp-boat striker. He said, "It was like I took a picture. I knew these people were dead. They wouldn't get out of their cars." At the last second, he ran back down the bridge. He was probably the biggest assistance we had in determining what vehicles were there that night. He could tell you every car and who was in it. It was frozen in his mind.

Another ship grazed the bridge a number of years later. The only fatality occurred a few months later when a friend of mine, one of the welders working on the repairs, went to slide down a beam that was torqued. They were cutting it, and the beam was still hot. He reached out and he hadn't "safetyed" off and reared back when he touched the beam. He fell about eighty feet and went down between the fender system and the bridge. Well, the current had cut a small channel under one of the pilings, and he got pushed up under the piling. They kept saying the current had taken him downriver. And I thought, *No. He's wearing forty to fifty pounds of gear.* So Jimmy Finn, a DNR [Georgia Department of Natural Resources] ranger, figured out that he had been pushed up under one of the feet. Of course, a lot of things had been pushed up under there. It's about forty-something feet deep there, and I spent about four hours searching. It made me a little nervous because I didn't have a backup diver. I only got stuck a few times, but I had plenty of air and a bailout bottle and a safety line. I had to fight the current and crawl up under the fender system and the edge of the bridge, and it was right tedious. I was one tired human being.

The visibility is double-damn zip down there. But I finally got lucky and found him. The problem was they wanted his climbing gear, to see if the safety line broke—which they never do; they just aren't buckled. So here's this big old boy, and I had to untangle him and drag him out of all the debris. Well, I had lost track of time and mentally began to think that I had to decompress. I got up on the piling to where I guessed the ten-foot line would be. I dragged him—literally, because he's so heavy—up the fender system, and I don't want to overinflate, since I want to stop and lay on that fender system for as long as I can stand it to make sure I decompress. Ninety-nine out of a hundred victims, I tie them to me so I don't lose him. But I realized that I might have to go back to get him because I was getting totally whipped. I wasn't 100 percent sure I could break the surface.

Finally, I thought, *It's time to blow or go*, so I got a hold of him by his belt. So I blew the surface, and it was screaming—raining and thundering. And I'm beating on the side of the ranger boat, but they can't hear me. So I slid down the boat, and I'm not a happy boy.

But this old man who lived up on Highway 17—a professional bridge builder, an old black man—he was friends with the victim, and he'd worked with me around shrimp boats on weekends. He's the hero of this deal. He told the bossman, "I'm going to stay right here until the diver gets him." So he got in a boat with a bottle of Gatorade and three or four packs of cigarettes and sat there. If it rained, he sat there. If it lightninged, he sat there. The second he saw the back of my head break the surface, he cast off and cranked up.

He came around the bridge, and I was gone by then. I thought, *If I'm lucky, I'll float to a little cut south of the bridge and wait in the shallow water until a shrimp boat comes by*. So there I am going down the river, and here he comes. He caught up with me and turned the boat sideways. I was so tired I couldn't get in the boat. He tied a rope around the decedent. I told the old man he could just dump me in the marsh with the victim, but he said, "Oh, no. I've known this youngun. We'll take him home." So we did. Finally, we got in the boat. He gave me the rest of his Gatorade, and I couldn't move. We idled back up to the bridge. Nobody but that old man had seen me break surface.

I had to inventory the decedent and put him in a body bag because the ranger lady was ill, which is understandable on your first extraction. And I had to puke about a quart of seawater. So I got him in the bag and said a little prayer over him. And I got into a little trouble. I'm sitting over the gunnels of the boat, eating a cheeseburger and drinking Gatorade and coffee. I had to eat something because I was dehydrated. One of the news guys gets a picture of me. But the family thanked me.

After a dive like that, you go to the emergency room and get stitched up. My face is covered in scars from running into stuff underwater. Then you go home and die. You get in the hot tub. You scrub all the places you're cut, burned, banged, broke. You wake up the next morning, and there isn't enough Advil in the world to stop the hurting. For about two days, you just want to hydrate. If you take this seriously, you play things over in your mind. That's how you learn.

After we got the bridge restored, we had a twenty-six-car pileup, and they all caught on fire one foggy morning. It was almost like that bridge was cursed with freak accidents and bridge jumpers. On the old bridge, you weren't but about forty feet above the water, so jumpers had to climb one of the four towers. One morning, there was a jumper in the southeast tower. We cornered him—a house painter—and kept talking to him. I finally got him to come to me. He agreed to come freely.

Another one was up about thirty feet in the southeast tower. I happened to be driving by and saw this young female city officer talking to him. I thought, *Uh-oh. Where's your backup, lady?* So I bailed out of the truck and ran over there. His girlfriend left him, and la-di-da. He broke in her house, stole the ring back, and he's holding this five-thousand-dollar diamond ring in his hand. The young lady officer is doing a half-decent job talking to him, but she's standing too close. I'm chewing on my cigar and listening to her. I don't want to interrupt her line of talk, but she's not doing so well. Matter of fact, he gets so distraught during the conversation that he says, "If she won't have this ring, nobody will." He turns around and chunks it in the river. She says, "Oh, my God!" That's when he decided to jump, and I'm thinking, *You could have given the ring to me!* So I grab for him, and by then another policeman—a young city policeman we call Rocky—had arrived. He'd been in the marines and was a heavyweight boxer. As I grabbed for the guy, he yelled, "Baker! Watch!" So I got between the lady officer and the jumper. And I could swear in court I never saw him hit that boy. Rocky told me later, "Mr. Baker, I dimed him twice." I said I could swear he hit his chin on the bridge rail. So we call the ambulance and take the guy away. And I'm looking at this young lady, and I said, "You're blessed, darlin', or you'd be down there in the water with that guy." We had a little course right then: "Don't get your ass too close to these people. You're trying to save them, not become a victim yourself."

The state reopened rights to bid on old heart-pine logs lying on the bottom of these rivers, which people building all these fancy houses will pay anything for. I won't do logging, though. There are tons of old logs on the river bottoms that were floated down from middle Georgia to the mills in Darien and on St. Simons over a hundred years ago.[2] That old-growth wood is extremely valuable now. I did some of that in Darien thirty-five years ago, but it's just too dangerous. You can get killed in a heartbeat doing that kind of work. Somebody's going to get killed trying to handle those cables underwater.

Over the years, I've come across a lot of things while looking for something else—airplanes, jewelry, ordnance–you name it. I've tripped over enough ordnance to fill up a tractor-trailer. Most of the time, we'll get a call to a bridge abutment to search for a victim or a weapon. It seems like everybody who was in the military swiped a piece of ordnance to impress their girlfriends or kill fish. They throw it off the bridge, and it doesn't go off. Here we divers come, stumbling along through the mud in the dark. If you have a little military background, you feel something like that and say to yourself, "Better not mess with this."

Supposedly, there are atomic weapons lost in the mud off the coast south of Tybee Island.[3] They haven't been found yet. It's my opinion that they're further down the coast. Anything that falls in the water and the sand around here is covered and uncovered, because the sand moves.

I spent a lot of years working in the ocean, where the shrimp boats would hang up on obstructions. Lee Howe, one of the locals, was a pilot instructor based on St. Simons during World War II and actually crashed an airplane off of the pier. Occasionally, a shrimper would drag up part of that engine. Probably the furthest I've gone offshore is sixty, maybe eighty miles, where the continental shelf drops off.

There are stories of collaborators here who would bury diesel fuel on the beaches of Cumberland during the war and would go out in the old shrimp boats and actually service the German U-boats. That's an oral tradition around the water here because everybody has known everybody else going way back. Off of St. Marys, bread wrappers and ticket stubs from the movie theaters here and in Jacksonville washed ashore. Bill Diehl wrote a book called *The Hunt*, which was about the twenty-seven millionaires on Jekyll Island.[4] I helped him with the technical aspects of it. It was about the Germans' plans to snatch the millionaires off of Jekyll with the U-boats and hold them hostage. In fact, the government made the millionaires leave Jekyll for fear that would happen.

For ages, the Spanish would sail cargo ships up the St. Mary's River to refurbish them and get the saltwater worms out of the wood, using the tannic acid in the fresh water. I came across a number of artifacts from one of the wrecks, a Spanish caravel or a galleon, while we were searching for a drowning victim. To give you an idea of the oddities that come out of the water here, years ago a friend of mine found a breastplate of Spanish armor excavating a spring in west Georgia near Valdosta.

Several people around here make a living harvesting prehistoric sharks' teeth out of the riverbanks.

We'll contact Jason Burns, the state underwater archaeologist based at the Skidaway Institute, if we come across graves that have fallen off a riverbank into the river. We try to get the names off the stones. We're rescue divers, so we just say a prayer over them. I don't care if it's an Indian grave or what, we don't exhume or bother the graves. It's just not decent. We make a point of not telling people where those places are.

I've come across buttons and belt buckles from the Civil War era and enough safes and guns to fill two trucks. These non-high-tech burglars break in with a wrecker and haul off the safe. Then they take it out in the boonies and burn it or blow it open and dump the safe in a pond or a bar [borrow] pit. Sooner or later, we'll find it. There's a very strong commonality among people who commit crimes and the way they do things. They think they're the most original rocket scientists there ever were and throw evidence in the water.

I know of a number of airplanes underwater around here— old navy planes, drug runners—in the Frederica, the Hampton [rivers]. We have a string of ten or twelve crashes in what's called the St. Andrews Triangle. Private pilots will spend a weekend in Jacksonville, usually at sporting events, and try to fly back to Atlanta, and the weather or the fog will get them. They'll get scared and try to shoot an approach into St. Simons off that old ILS [navigation beacon] off the Jekyll causeway, and they just disappear. I've been fortunate enough to help some families get a little closure over the last fifteen years. With the help of shrimp boaters, we will get a report about a hang [underwater obstruction]. Over time, the thing [a plane] will get banged and franged. Usually, what you come out with looks like the world's biggest ball of tinfoil. There's little or no bone residue left because the small predators eat the bones right out of the wreckage.

I did a commercial salvage in a golf course pond twenty years ago. All the lady's jewelry went in a pond. We also helped recover some of the [space shuttle] *Challenger*'s parts when it went down. We once helped retrieve a nose cone off of an AT&T satellite. It looked like a humongous pencil eraser, bigger than a car. At first, AT&T didn't want it back. Being a telephone man—I worked for BellSouth then—we cut it up into little pieces and made souvenirs. Then we found they wanted it back. Too late.

I've come across old cars—Model A's, debilitated wrecks from logging operations, things like that. When you find a car that old in the water, it's in pieces, strewn up and down a riverbank or a lake.

Carl Alexander, who used to be the Glynn County chief of police, is one of my original rescue divers. He started out as a volunteer fireman before he was a police officer. I once saw him jump into a burning airplane and rescue some people. They all lived. I knew enough about planes and didn't have the courage. He dragged us in there and made us help him. Any number of times, Chief Carl would show up at an accident site while off-duty on a Sunday and come charging up there and get right there in the middle of it with us.

We find ballast islands all the time. Ships would anchor out in the channel and throw the ballast stones overboard. In the old days, people would salvage the ballast. They cut paths out along the riverbank and used mule teams to drag the river for the ballast. They'd bore holes through the ballast and drag them back to the docks to be reused. Once, I found one of those stones. Visualize a humongous bowling ball with a hole through it and some engraved writing on it, weighing thirty or forty pounds. I took it home because no living room is complete without a big rock with a hole through it. I gave it to a friend of mine, Chrissie Halderson. So she takes it to Little St. Simons, where she was working. One night, this professor from Pennsylvania was visiting there and sees that rock. He whips out his checkbook and tells her it is a Viking rock, left behind by the Vikings way back when. About three years later, I'm diving around another shrimp boat at the docks and find another rock. I haul the rock and put it on the dock. This old black gentleman was fishing there and said, "What are you going to do with that rock?" I told him I was going to give it to a girlfriend of mine. He says, "I'd like to have it. It reminds me of my great-granddaddy. He was a mule skinner, and that's a ballast rock. That hole was to put the chain through. He'd drag them back down to the other end of town and sell them to the ships." Then he pointed to some engraving on the rock and said, "See that mark right there? That's my granddaddy's cousin's." It was part of old ballast that was once piled up on a dock until it wasn't needed anymore. Each person had a certain mark he'd pound on the rock. So Chrissie sold that professor a rock worth about ten dollars, not a Viking heirloom.

I have made a number of dives at Ebo's Landing. Its exact location is probably not where people think it is. I have found any number of old chains around there, but they could be old logging chains. Many of the chains in logging operations look like shackles. I've spent thirty-five years getting chains off of propellers and out of docks. I can take a good, modern steel-grade chain, leave it under a dock for five years, and an expert may testify that it is a hundred years old. One argument is that Ebo's Landing was at the very head of that creek behind Longview Shopping Center. But that creek has moved drastically, according to some old charts I've observed. My best guess is that the actual Ebo's Landing is at the end of Glynn Haven somewhere in the marsh.

The thing that made *The Wanderer* [the last ship that brought slaves from Africa to the United States] special was that they accidentally built a sailing vessel that would practically plane, it was so fast. Today, we would call it a planing hull. And it didn't draw that much water. That's why it was used to haul slaves.

On one dive in the Altamaha, where someone's nets were snagged on a hang, I found some old French brandy that was still potable. They were round, greenish glass bottles with what looked like some kind of foil covering the cork. Right there near Darien, where we found the bottles, is the d'Antignac family, whose lineage goes way back. Legend has it that they were good friends of Napoleon and that the last time he took it on the lam, he sent two sloops ahead with his personal supplies. One made it. The other one sank. Legend also has it—and Jack d'Antignac lives in the same house—that the family was waiting for Napoleon to come hide out with them.[5]

The Stevenses and the Taylors were all related [see the Sarah "Sally" Elizabeth Taylor Jones and Dr. Charles E. Pearson narrative]. These guys fought in the Spanish-American War and World Wars I and II. I used to go visit Captain Doug Taylor on his front porch. He was about in his nineties then. They made him swear off smoking, so he chewed tobacco. He was about crippled by arthritis by then, but he was a hell of a man. He had been a boat driver and managed Little St. Simons Island for years. When Sea Palms [Golf Resort] got going, they were in a feud with several people over property they bought. So they brought Captain Doug out of retirement. Six young, strong men carried him out in the marsh in a rattan chair. He sat there in his chair and pointed to where he wanted to go, and they carried him out in the marsh in the middle of nowhere. He hadn't been there since he was a little boy eighty years before. He looked around the marsh and trees—they call them "lineups"—and he said, "The stake is right here." Lo and behold, they dug down and found the stone marker. Sea Palms won the case.

Mr. Stevens' family used to own Fort Frederica lock, stock, and barrel. He was a surveyor and a well driller. When he wanted to hide something, he'd get out his transit, measure an area, and dig a hole eight feet deep in the middle of the night. Then he'd wrap whatever it was he was going to bury in a canvas and Cosmoline [a rust preventative]. That's the way he hid things. He didn't believe in banks. Bless his heart, he didn't think he was going to die as soon as he did, or he would have gotten around to telling someone where they are. I asked his daughter about it awhile back, and she said he never told anyone where he buried them.

Somewhere in the ground at Frederica or under Longview Shopping Center, probably under concrete, is a bunch of green ledgers, and the history of the islands is in those ledgers.

NOTES

1. *Brunswick News*, November 8, 2004.

2. Orrin Sage Wightman and Margaret Davis Cate, *Early Days of Coastal Georgia* (St. Simons Island, Ga.: Fort Frederica Association, 1955), 147. The authors note that "the long-leaf yellow pine which supplied this [Hilton and Dodge Lumber Company] mill was cut in the interior of Georgia and floated down the Altamaha River in great rafts."

3. Tony Bartelme, *Post and Courier* (Charleston, S.C.), February 8, 2004. Bartelme reports that "on the frigid night of Feb. 5, 1958, Maj. Howard Richardson's hands warmed the controls of a B-47 Stratojet. . . . In the plane's belly was the Mark 15, serial number 47782, about 11 feet long and weighing 7,600 pounds. . . . Richardson guided his crippled warplane toward Hunter Air Force Base near Savannah, . . . turned the plane out to sea and let the bomb go."

4. William Diehl, *The Hunt* (New York: Ballantine Books, 1991).

5. Don W. Farrant, *The Lure and Lore of the Golden Isles* (Nashville, Tenn.: Rutledge Hill Press, 1993), 72. The author writes that "in 1820 . . . there was a plot to smuggle Napoleon out of St. Helena, where he'd been exiled, to America. French sympathizers had selected three locations in the United States, and one of them was the [d'Antignac] house in McIntosh County."

Select Bibliography

Allen, Benjamin. *Glynn County, Georgia: Black America Series*. Charleston, S.C.: Arcadia Publishing, 2003.

Anderson, William. *The Wild Man from Sugar Creek: The Political Career of Eugene Talmadge*. Baton Rouge: Louisiana State University Press, 1975.

Barefoot, Patricia. *Falling for Coastal Magic: Stories of Southeast Georgia*. St. Simons Island, Ga.: Saltmarsh Press, 1998.

Bell, Malcolm, Jr. *Major Butler's Legacy*. Athens: University of Georgia Press, 1987.

Cate, Margaret Davis. *Our Todays and Yesterdays: A Story of Brunswick and the Coastal Islands*. Spartanburg, S.C.: The Reprint Company, Publishers, 1999.

Conner, Judson J. *Muskets, Knives and Bloody Marshes: The Fight for Colonial Georgia*. St. Simons Island, Ga.: Saltmarsh Press, 2001.

Farrant, Don W. *The Lure and Lore of the Golden Isles*. Nashville, Tenn.: Rutledge Hill Press, 1993.

Georgia Writers' Project. *Drums and Shadows*. Athens: University of Georgia Press, 1940.

Ginn, Edwin H. *The First Hundred Years: A History of the American National Bank of Brunswick*. Brunswick, Ga.: Glover Printing Company, 1989.

Graham, Abbie Fuller. *Old Mill Days: St. Simons Mills, Georgia, 1874–1908*. Brunswick, Ga.: St. Simons Public Library, Glover Printing Company, 1976.

Greene, Melissa Faye. *Praying for Sheetrock*. New York: Fawcett Columbine, Ballantine Books, 1991.

Kemble, Frances Ann. *Journal of a Residence on a Georgian Plantation in 1838–1839*. 1863. Reprint, Athens: University of Georgia Press, 1984.

Kimsey, Thora Olsen, and Sonja Olsen Kinard. *Memories from The Marshes of Glynn: World War II*. Decatur, Ga.: Looking Glass Books, 1999.

Lovell, Caroline Couper. *The Golden Isles of Georgia*. Boston: Little, Brown and Company, 1933.

——. *The Light of Other Days*. Macon, Ga.: Mercer University Press, 1995.

Marye, Florence. *The Story of the Page-King Family of Retreat Plantation, St. Simons Island and of the Golden Isles of Georgia*. Edited by Edwin R. MacKethan III. Darien, Ga.: Darien Printing and Graphics, 2000.

McFeely, William S. *Sapelo's People: A Long Walk into Freedom*. New York and London: W. W. Norton, 1994.

Milanich, Jerald T. *Laboring in the Fields of the Lord*. Washington and London: Smithsonian Institution Press, 1999.

Moore, Francis. *A Voyage to Georgia, Begun in the Year 1735*. Vol. 1. 1744. Reprint, St. Simons Island, Ga.: Fort Frederica Association, 1983.

Morris, Patricia. *St. Simons Island*. Charleston, S.C.: Arcadia Publishing, 2003.

Morrison, Carlton. *Running the River: Poleboats, Steamboats & Timber Rafts on the Altamaha, Ocmulgee, Oconee & Ohoopee*. St. Simons Island, Ga.: Saltmarsh Press, 2003.

Ottley, Roi. *The Lonely Warrior: The Life and Times of Robert S.*

Abbott. Chicago: Henry Regnery Company, 1955.

Schoettle, Taylor, and Jennifer Smith. *A Naturalist's Guide to St. Simons Island*. Darien, Ga.: *Darien News*, 1993.

Vanstory, Burnette. *Georgia's Land of the Golden Isles*. Athens: Brown Thrasher Books, University of Georgia Press, 1956.

Wightman, Orrin Sage, and Margaret Davis Cate. *Early Days of Coastal Georgia*. St. Simons Island, Ga.: Fort Frederica Association, 1955.

Wood, Virginia Steele. *Live Oaking: Southern Timber for Tall Ships*. Boston: Northeastern University Press, 1981.

Worth, John. *The Struggle for the Georgia Coast: An Eighteenth-Century Spanish Retrospective on Guale and Mocama*. New York and Athens: American Museum of Natural History, University of Georgia Press, 1995.

Roamer, Charles, 233-34
Roamer, Katherine, 233-34
Rooks, Burnette, 34
Rooks, Emory, 38
Rooks, Joann, 38
Rooks, Winfred, 38
Roosevelt, Franklin D., 12, 67-68, 142
Roxy Theatre, 221
Ryals, Abraham, Jr., 11
Ryals, Abraham, Sr., 11, 12
Ryals, Ernest Lee, 9
Ryals, Sadie Marie Jackson, 3

Sali-bul-Ali, 31
Salzburgers, 123
Sapelo Island, 136, 137, 184, 211, 212, 214-16, 230
Sapelo Island Cultural and Revitalization Society, 215
Sausage, Doc, 222
Scotland, Ga., 140
Scott, Charlton, 42
Sea Island, 22, 58, 122, 124, 184, 185
Sea Island Clubhouse, 88
Sea Island Company, 79, 110, 114, 136, 139, 143, 144, 149, 212
Sea Island Fish Camp, 122
Sea Island Golf Course, 77, 79, 145, 220, 221
Sea Island Road, 147
Sea Island Singers, 92
Sea Island Yacht Club, 132, 136, 159, 161, 164
Sea Palms (Resort), 147, 219, 222, 245
Seldon Park, 40, 77
Sengstacke, Robert Abbott, 99
Seymour, Carnell, 225
Shadman, 149

Shepherd, Ellen, 148
Sidney Lanier Bridge, 177, 187-89, 201, 229, 235-39
Sidney Lanier Elementary School, 133, 178
Simmons, 120
Skidaway Institute, 242
Small, Billy, 152
Small, Charlotte Galing, 79
Small, Clarence, 79
Small, Clementine, 79
Small, Cornelia, 79
Small, Ila, 79
Small, Leanora, 79
Small, Louturia, 79
Small, Neptune, Jr., 71, 79-80, 88, 147, 222
South End, 152, 216-17, 221
Spalding, Thomas, 83
Stallings, 178
St. Andrews Sound, 159
St. Andrews Triangle, 242
St. Francis School, 19
St. Francis Xavier Church, 19
St. Ignatius Episcopal Church, 37, 145, 146
St. James Lutheran Church, 164
St. Luke Church, 214
St. Marys, Ga., 206, 241
St. Mary's River, 241
St. Paul Missionary Baptist Church, 81, 145, 151
St. Simons Hotel, 60, 92, 201
St. Simons Elementary School, 105, 133
St. Simons Little Theatre, 204
Stevens (family), 26, 77, 104, 172, 245
Stevens, Charles, 96, 103, 104, 106, 111, 112, 113
Stevens, Elliott, 122

CPSIA information can be obtained at www.ICGtesting.com
Printed in the USA
BVOW08s1457190614

356789BV00008B/34/P